T0331075

Schema Coaching

Schema Coaching is an informative guide for coaches, providing readers with a powerful and evidence-based approach to dealing with persistent personal difficulties.

Schema coaching has a strong foundation in schema therapy which has been used in many parts of the world for over 20 years as a highly successful approach for helping clients with anxiety and depression, as well as more severe personality disorders. The book provides clear practical guidelines, illustrative case studies and reflective practice exercises to those who wish to implement a range of schema techniques when coaching with the non-clinical population. The book is in two parts, the first is primarily designed for coaches that do not have clinical, counselling or psychotherapy training and the second includes more advanced techniques which are designed for coaches with this type of training or qualifications. It also clearly sets out the ethical steps any coach should undertake before using therapeutic techniques with a client.

This will be an informative and engaging resource in a new and extremely important area of coaching, suitable for coaches, coaching psychologists, coaching educators and anyone with a general interest in this topic.

Iain McCormick is the founder of the Executive Coaching Centre in Auckland, New Zealand. He trained in clinical psychology, subsequently completing a PhD in work stress. Iain has coached and consulted for 30 years, in Canada, Hong Kong and New Zealand. He is an award-winning executive coach and author.

Coaching Psychology

Series Editor: Stephen Palmer

Coaching psychology is a distinct branch of academic and applied psychology that focuses on enhancement of performance, development and wellbeing in the broader population. Written by leading experts, the **Coaching Psychology** series will highlight innovations in the field, linking theory, research and practice. These books will interest professionals from psychology, coaching, mentoring, business, health, human resources and management as well as those interested in the psychology underpinning their coaching and mentoring practice.

Titles in the series:

https://www.routledge.com/Coaching-Psychology/book-series/COACHPSYCH

Schema Coaching

Overcoming Deep-seated Challenges

Iain McCormick

Routledge
Taylor & Francis Group

LONDON AND NEW YORK

Designed cover image: © Getty Images. Natrot. Abstract colorful geometrical background

First published 2025
by Routledge
4 Park Square, Milton Park, Abingdon, Oxon OX14 4RN

and by Routledge
605 Third Avenue, New York, NY 10158

Routledge is an imprint of the Taylor & Francis Group, an informa business

© 2025 Iain McCormick

British Library Cataloguing-in-Publication Data
A catalogue record for this book is available from the British Library

Library of Congress Cataloging-in-Publication Data
A catalog record has been requested for this book

ISBN: 978-1-032-81875-7 (hbk)
ISBN: 978-1-032-81874-0 (pbk)
ISBN: 978-1-003-50182-4 (ebk)

DOI: 10.4324/9781003501824

Typeset in Times New Roman
by Taylor & Francis Books

Contents

Illustrations

About the Author

Iain McCormick PhD is the founder of the Executive Coaching Centre in Auckland, New Zealand. He initially trained in clinical psychology, working in the forensic sector, and subsequently completed his PhD studying work stress during a long overland traverse of Antarctica. Iain then moved into organisational consulting and coaching, becoming a Partner in Deloitte for some years, working in Canada and New Zealand. He subsequently moved to Hong Kong, where he helped build a consulting firm that was sold to a US multinational. Iain returned to New Zealand in 2000 and started the Executive Coaching Centre. He currently coaches a wide range of boards of directors, chief executives and senior managers. He has conducted many thousands of individual and team coaching sessions over 30 years. Iain has been running schema coaching sessions since 2014 with the assistance of both a coaching supervisor and a schema therapy supervisor. Over the years, he has benefited greatly from undertaking a range of schema therapy to deal with his own personal challenges. He is a Fellow of the New Zealand Psychological Society and has published a wide range of articles and books on coaching, organisational psychology and psychometrics.

Foreword for Schema Coaching: Overcoming Deep-Seated Challenges

Over the past two decades the fields of coaching and coaching psychology practice have gained traction as important evidence-based interventions that can be applied in organisations, communities, families, health settings and for people wanting to achieve their personal and life goals. Occasionally advanced techniques taken from the therapeutic field are used to enable understanding, insight and facilitate change.

Schema coaching was originally derived from schema therapy. In this book, Dr Iain McCormick demonstrates how schema coaching techniques can be used by coaches and coaching psychologists to help people to overcome deep-rooted challenges. The schema occasionally seen in coaching are listed as unrelenting striving, sense of failure, needing approval, self-sacrifice and lack of support. These schemas are often issues that most coaches and coaching psychologists will have encountered with some of their coachees, yet just using the more usual coaching frameworks or models may seem ineffective. This is the bridge linking standard coaching skills and techniques to schema coaching in order to facilitate a journey of discovery and goal achievement.

As coaches may have a range of experience and training, the book has been divided in two parts, where the first is principally designed for coaches who do not have relevant therapeutic training and the second for more therapeutically qualified coaches which includes more advanced schema coaching techniques. The book highlights that careful consideration of the risks and ethical issues involved in the practice of schema coaching is central to the use of these techniques and coaches need ongoing, regular, documented supervision with a senior well-trained professional.

The chapters include useful illustrative case studies, reflective practice exercises, key learning points, group discussion and suggested reading. This enables the reader to reflect on their understanding of the topic being discussed.

This insightful book will provide practitioners with an opportunity to learn more about the developing field of schema coaching and its application.

Professor Stephen Palmer PhD FISCP Series Editor, Coaching Psychology

With gratitude

I am deeply grateful to my wife, Kerry, and my two sons, Cam and Olly. I also thank my clients for the courage and willingness to work with me. Finally, I am indebted to Emeritus Professor Tony Taylor (1926–2021), my great teacher, mentor and dear friend.

Author's Note

The examples, case studies and anecdotes provided in this book are drawn loosely from my coaching, consulting and teaching conducted over many years. Names and a wide range of identifying details about these people have been changed to protect their privacy. Many of the case studies in this book are composites drawn from a range of different clients, students and contacts seen over the course of my work. Any resemblance in the case studies to actual persons is entirely coincidental.

Chapter 1

The nature of coaching

This chapter presents the purpose and structure of the book and then examines coaching and how it works. Coaching is a collaborative solution-focused process in which the coach helps clients to enhance their life and reach their personal and professional goals. It is a rapidly growing profession that offers a wide range of assistance to a great variety of individuals. There are many different approaches to coaching and many books have been written on the topic. This chapter outlines four popular books in the area and uses these to draw up a set of common threads that characterise the process. The chapter also includes an illustrative case study, a reflective practice exercise for the reader, a summary of key learning points, discussion topics and suggested further reading on this topic.

The purpose and structure of the book

The purpose of this book is to introduce the trained, supervised and ethically adherent coach, coaching psychologist or coaching educator to the schema coaching approach. While the book frequently uses the term 'coach' the focus is primarily but not exclusively for coaching psychologists. It will also be of value to a wide range of general readers with an interest in the use of therapeutic approaches in coaching. Schema coaching is derived from schema therapy (McCormick, 2022) and it is designed to be used with individuals from the non-clinical population who typically have a reasonable degree of psychological, social and vocational stability. Schema coaching includes a range of advanced techniques and so needs to be approached with caution and only after a careful consideration of risks and ethical issues involved (McCormick, 2023a).

The book is in two parts, the first is primarily designed for coaches that do not have clinical, counselling or psychotherapy training and the second includes more advanced techniques which are primarily designed for coaches with this training or qualifications.

The book includes chapters on:

1 The nature of coaching
2 Using therapeutic tools in coaching

DOI: 10.4324/9781003501824-1

Introduction to coaching

The coaching profession is growing extremely rapidly, all around the globe. The number of practitioners worldwide exceeded 100,000 in 2022. This is an increase of 54 per cent since 2019. The total estimated revenue generated is US$4.5 billion, a 60 per cent increase since 2020 with growth particularly robust in Asia, the Middle East, Africa, and Eastern Europe (ICF, 2023).

One reason for this growth is the development of many different types of coaches who assist clients with diverse challenges including: attention deficit hyperactivity disorder coaches, business and executive coaches, career coaches, dating coaches, finance coaches, health coaches, homework coaches, life coaches, relationship coaches, sports coaches, vocal coaches and writing coaches (Wikipedia, 2024a).

So, what is coaching? A giant in the profession, Tony Grant, described coaching as a "collaborative solution-focused, result-orientated and systematic process in which the coach facilitates the enhancement of life experience and goal attainment in the personal and/or professional life of normal, non-clinical clients" (Grant, 2003, p. 254).

Four great coaching books

To further understand the nature of coaching, I draw upon four books that have impacted me in my 30 years of executive coaching. These are:

1 The brilliant little book *Coaching plain and simple: Solution-focused brief coaching essentials*, by Peter Szabó and Daniel Meier (Szabó & Meier, 2009).

2   The fascinatingly simple best seller *The coaching habit: Say less, ask more & change the way you lead forever*, by Michael Bungay Stanier (Stanier, 2016).
3   The well-researched *Helping people change: Coaching with compassion for lifelong learning and growth* by Richard Boyatzis and colleagues (Boyatzis et al., 2019).
4   The leading edge *Third wave cognitive behavioural coaching: contextual, behavioural and neuroscience approaches for evidence based coaches*, edited by Jonathan Passmore and Sarah Leach (Passmore & Leach, 2022).

Coaching plain and simple: Solution-focused brief coaching essentials

This easy-to-read book first came out in 2008 and outlines the key steps in coaching. The approach used, solution-focused coaching, was developed out of solution-focused brief therapy which is a strengths-based approach founded over 20 years ago (Szabó & Meier, 2009). A summary of the steps in rapid solution-focused coaching are set out below.

Step 1: The coaching agreement

The first step in this type of coaching involves the coach and client agreeing on what success in coaching looks like. The coach may ask 'What do you want from our coaching sessions?' 'What do you want to achieve in this first session?' 'If our coaching went really well over the next year, what would you tell me about the changes you made?' If the client is rather resistant to these questions and can only talk about what they don't want – a useful question is 'So can we now take what you don't and flip it into a list of what you do want?' For clients with complex challenges, it can be useful to ask, 'You have talked about a range of challenges – where shall we start our coaching?' The conclusion of this first step is the client and coach agreeing on the outcome of the coaching.

Step 2: The preferred future

Clients typically arrive at coaching focused on their challenges or problems. Simply staying with the challenge or problem often does not resolve much. Solution-focused coaching sidesteps this problem and asks the client what would happen if it disappeared. This can either be called the *miracle* question 'Suppose you woke up tomorrow and something magic had happened so you felt deeply contented what would you then do?' or sometimes the *what if* question 'What if your boss started to acknowledge your work, what would you do?' Both these preferred future questions enable the client to feel a sense of distance and relief from the problem and to focus on the future. Great coaches are never satisfied with a simplistic answer to these questions, they dig in and explore the detail of exactly what this ideal future or ideal self looks like. Experienced coaches often use the word *suppose* at the start of the preferred future questions so that the client does not get side tracked in discussion about possible obstacles such as not having enough money or time or motivation. These questions help the client connect with all a hopeful solution-focused future.

Step 3: Precursors of the solution

This phase explores the small steps that the client has already taken to solve the problem or to move forward any distance. The coach could ask 'How have you dealt with this situation in the past?', or, 'What steps have you already taken to overcome this challenge?' If the client is somewhat resistant and keeps talking about the problem the coach can turn the situation around and into something positive by saying 'Gee I can see how big this issue is, I am really impressed with the determination and resilience that you have clearly shown' or 'Given the stress, I really admire your confidence to continue'. At this stage sincere complements are very powerful in convincing the client that they have done well to get this far with the challenge.

The use of scaling questions at this point in the coaching is also important. A coach can ask, 'On a scale from 1 being totally stuck to 10 being totally solved – where are you at the moment?'. If this client says 2 on the scale, the coach can ask 'That is great, and what have you done to move up from 1?'.

The purpose of this step in the coaching is to demonstrate to the client that despite having a significant problem, they have already made some progress. Once this is established, the coaching can move on to further explore future options.

Step 4: Clues for upcoming progress

After the scaling question has been used the coach can ask 'You said that you are currently at 2. What would you need to do to get to 3 on the scale?' Good coaches choose their words carefully and do not ask 'Can you take the next step?' as the client may answer 'No way'. So, the coach will ask 'What would help you to move to step 4?'. Clients can be overly optimistic and start setting themselves impossible targets at this point. The coach may say 'Running a marathon next month would be brilliant, but shall we start with a goal of a half marathon in three months' time?'. Small realistic steps are critical to progress in coaching.

When the client starts exploring options for future steps forward, the coach can reinforce then and ensure that there are multiple possible options, just in case one does not work out. The purpose of this step and the generation of options are to help the client to see that the future is open to a wide range of possible new positive ways forward.

Step 5: Session conclusion

Towards the end of the session there are several issues that can be addressed by the coach which include:

- Does the client want to talk about anything else in the session?
- How close is the client to reaching the goal for the session?
- The coach can reinforce progress and complement the client on it.
- They can agree on the date of the next session.
- They can finalise the client's action plan.

In conclusion, I have used this solution-focused approach for many years and I find it extremely helpful as it enables me to generate powerful, practical, future-focused questions to move the coaching forward.

The coaching habit: Say less, ask more and change the way you lead forever

Michael Bungay Stanier's book (Stanier, 2016) is a stripped down, simple, easy read that is focused on seven questions that are primarily relevant in coaching by managers, but these are also useful for professional coaches.

Question 1: The kickstart question

According to Stanier a great place to start coaching is with 'What is on your mind?' This open question is particularly useful to begin the coaching process if the coach or manager is not sure where to start. It gets the conversation going, helps to show interest in the client and builds trust. It does not start the conversation off with advice or guidance but with genuine curiosity and interest. This approach says, 'Let's chat about what is important to you'.

To help the individual move forward it can be useful to focus on the 3Ps and ask about challenges in the:

- Projects that the person is involved in.
- People that they work with.
- Patterns of behaviour or ways of working that can be improved.

The purpose of this kickstart question is to begin the coaching in an open manner that encourages the client to talk about what is important to them.

Question 2: The AWE question

The kickstart will get the conversation going but it may not demonstrate what the most important issue is. The AWE – And What Else question – helps to uncover other important things that the person wants to talk about. It is the beginning of uncovering important problems but also important solutions. The AWE is useful as it generates a deeper conversation, stops the coach giving advice and gives the coach time to listen and think.

At this stage there are four practical things that the coach can do to help support the process:

- Stay curious and genuine.
- Ask one question at a time.
- Recognise success.
- Move on when ready.

The purpose of the AWE question is to begin a deeper conversation and to stop the coach giving unwanted advice.

Question 3: The focus question

At this point in the coaching the aim is to find the central issue or problem that the person has. Stanier suggests that asking the question 'What is the most important challenge right now?' will help to clarify this. It is critical that the focus at this time is not on the first problem that the client presents but on their real or most important challenge. This helps to cut through the fog of issues. If the person brings up a topic that involves or blames someone else, it can be helpful to use the focus question to bring the conversation back to what the individual can control right now.

Using this type of question, the coach moves from advice giving and performance discussions about everyday problem solving to development coaching which is about growth and solving important future issues. There are three strategies that can help:

- Trusting that the developmental coaching process will be useful, even if the manager or coach feels concerned about this issue at the start.
- Understanding that it can be helpful, sometimes, to give advice but this should not be the first response from the coach.
- Repeating the AWE question can enable the conversation to go deeper.

Question 4: The foundation question

The question 'What do you want?' is at the heart of this book. Most people find this hard to answer and even if they do know what they want, they are reluctant to say it.

It can take courage to ask and to answer.

It is useful for the coach to separate out wants 'I would like this' and needs 'I must have this'. Wants are surface issues and can include wanting more information, better cooperation and so on. Needs are requests at a much deeper level and can include affection, freedom, participation, creation, identification, protection and understanding. Effective coaching gets to the needs level because this represents the driving force for safety, change and personal development. Coaches need to listen with great care to understand the world of the client and develop deep powerful communication. Silence is an indication that the client is thinking deeply and perhaps grappling with what they really want. Effective coaches bite their tongues and don't jump into the silence. The length of the silence can be a measure of success. The clearer the client can express what they want, the more powerful the coaching.

The purpose of this question is to help the client identify their real needs so that subsequent coaching can focus on this.

Question 5: The lazy question

The lazy question is 'How can I help?'. It will enable the coach to not only be focused but to work less, because the client will decide what is most helpful to them. This question is beneficial because the coach is gently challenging the client to provide a clear and direct statement on what they need. It means the coach does not have to guess at what the best option for help is. It also inhibits advice giving.

When the client gives their answer, the coach has several options:

1   'Yes, I can do that' – a simple agreement.
2   'No, I can't do that' is another obvious option but it needs an explanation as to why – this is particularly relevant if the client wants something extreme such as to totally stop feeling sad, anxious, etc.
3   'I can't do that... but I could do something else' is a middle ground option which gives the client some more choices.
4   'Let me think about that.' Which buys the coach some time or perhaps 'I'm not sure – I'll need to check a few things out'.

The purpose of the lazy question is to help the client to decide what is most helpful to them at this point in the coaching conversation.

Question 6: The strategic question

This question is 'If you say Yes to this action, what are you saying No to?'. While this may appear most relevant in the context of the manager as coach, it is also relevant to the professional coach. It is easy for anyone, including our clients, to endlessly add items to their To Do lists and so achieve less and feel worse. The strategy question encourages the client to be realistic about their time and energy. Picking a small number of things to work on and succeeding in doing them is a critical part of coaching that is supported by the strategy question.

Question 7: The learning question

This question is 'From what we have discussed what was been most useful to you?' Coaching is about learning and this is unlikely to take place unless the client makes the time to pause, reflect and realise what they will do differently in future. The learning question encourages the client to undertake this reflection and so to grow.

In conclusion, I find this a fascinating set of questions that are an interesting contrast to the solution-focused model outlined above. I use this set of questions mostly when I am working more informally with a client rather than in a designated coaching session.

Helping people change: Coaching with compassion for lifelong learning and growth

This book was written by Richard Boyatzis and colleagues (Boyatzis et al., 2019). Boyatzis is Professor, Organizational Behavior, Weatherhead School of Management. He has a deeply impressive record of research and writing in coaching, leadership, competencies, emotional intelligence, neuroscience and management education.

The key ideas in the book are set out below.

Coaches inspire

Boyatzis and his colleagues are clear that inspiring, encouraging and supporting clients to help them to achieve their full potential is the purpose of coaching. This is called 'coaching with compassion' and is contrasted with 'coaching for compliance' which involves moving the client towards an externally imposed goal – usually a performance standard set by the person's manager. Coaching for compassion is achieved by developing a resonate relationship, that is, an authentic, positive, caring approach which inspires the client to grow.

The ideal self

Coaching with compassion involves helping the client to describe his or her ideal self and their own vision of their future. This positive, forward looking, aspirational approach to coaching sets an important tone. It is achieved by assisting the client to draw a sharp distinction between their 'ideal' self and their 'ought' self with the latter being driven by others' expectations of what ought to be. To build self-awareness the coach can introduce the personal balance sheet which is an exercise to set out the client's strengths and weakness in relation to their personal vision statement. This can be used to help the client map out a set of action to help them grow towards their ideal self.

These actions can then be practiced to the point of overlearning, so they become natural and spontaneous.

Positive emotional activation

By focusing on a positive path of growth and exploring the ideal self, the coach stimulates the client's parasympathetic nervous system or what Boyatzis calls the positive emotional activator (PEA). By contrast, focusing on inadequacies and asking negative questions will stimulate the less helpful stress response called the negative emotional activator (NEA). Coaching uses the PEA to help the client to be positive, hopeful, open to new ideas and more willing to change.

Thriving

The coach is encouraged to focus on the PEA two to five times more frequently than the NEA. This positive focus builds a sense of hope and renewal which is reinforced by regularly practicing relevant actions such as balancing time for rest and recuperation with time for concentration and deep work.

Personal vision

Coaching helps the client to draw up a comprehensive picture of their ideal self which is developed by exploring their dreams, purpose and core values. This personal aspiration is not a set of goals but a positive, enduring, direction of travel which is highly meaningful and important.

The resonate relationship

This powerful positive, caring, compassionate relationship between coach and client, with its shared vision of success, is at the core of coaching. Building up this relationship and helping the client move towards their ideal self takes time. Boyatzis encourages the coach to focus on the client and not on their problem or on any type of formulaic coaching process. Deep, sensitive, active listening by the coach supports and fosters the resonate relationship.

Coaching inside organisations

The book not only focuses on the one-on-one coaching relationship but also on how a coaching culture can be introduced in organisations. The latter can be done by encouraging staff to work in pairs to coach each other, by training management to coach their direct reports and by providing external professional coaches to staff.

Coachable moments

Boyatzis and colleagues suggest that it is important to find the moments when the client is most receptive to coaching. Identifying the times when the client is open and ready to reflect, learn and grow is critical to the personal and professional development of the client.

Research behind the ideas

Boyatzis has developed an impressive research base behind this approach to coaching and change. In a recent example, fMRI neuroimaging was used to examine the brains of individuals as they responded to two different styles of coaching – one focused on their "ideal self", that is the person they wanted to be and the other on their "real self", that is the person they were (Boyatzis et al., 2019). The research showed that when coaching focuses on someone's immediate problems this constrains their ability to see future possibilities. However, when the coaching was focused on the ideal self the individual experienced more positive emotion, were more open to new ideas and more intrinsically motivated (Boyatzis et al., 2023).

In conclusion, this book provides a logical and well researched approach to coaching that emphasises the identification of the ideal self and the asking of positive open questions within a resonate relationship to help the client move in their desired direction.

Third wave cognitive behavioural coaching: contextual, behavioural and neuroscience approaches for evidence-based coaches.

This book, edited by Jonathan Passmore and Sarah Leach, (Passmore & Leach, 2022), expands the reach of coaching by focusing on a range of therapeutic techniques that can be used in coaching with an emphasis on the most recently developed or third wave therapies. These therapeutic approaches have in common: a focus on the value of the relationship between the client's thinking, emotion and behaviour, the significance of the client's personal core values and identity and the importance of being able to identify and choose which thoughts and emotions to act upon.

The book is intended for experienced, trained, ethically adherent coaches who wish to use evidence-based approaches and to extend the range of options used in their coaching practice. The book illustrates how far coaching has come from the early days of solution-focused coaching and how coaches are now using advanced approaches integrating cognitive models of change.

The chapters in this book cover the use of the following therapeutic approaches:

- Cognitive behavioural coaching
- Cognitive behavioural chairwork
- Mindfulness and coaching
- Compassionate mind coaching
- Acceptance and commitment coaching
- Dialectical behavioural coaching
- Schema coaching
- Metacognitive approaches
- Neuroscience-based coaching
- Motivational interviewing coaching

This book contains a great depth of information and approaches, which means that a more in-depth discussion is not possible within the limited scope of this chapter

The common themes in these coaching books

These three books approach the topic of coaching in very different ways, yet they have a great deal in common and this is summarised below.

- The focus of coaching is on solutions not problems.
  - In *Solution-Focused Coaching* this emphasis is clear as soon as anyone reads the title.
  - In *The Coaching Habit* the Focus Question is designed to move the coach from advice giving to development coaching which is about finding solutions for growth and solving important future issues.
  - In *Helping People Change* it is suggested that the coach begins by helping the client to explore their ideal self and to clearly articulate a compelling personal vision as a basis for finding solutions to future personal growth.
  - In *Third Wave Cognitive Behavioural Coaching* the coach learns that there are many different modern evidence-based pathways to co-developing client solutions.

- The coach helps facilitate the development capability of the client rather than to give advice or to understand the origin of the problem.
  - In *Solution-Focused Coaching* an early focus is on the client's preferred solution rather than on the cause of the problem.
  - In *The Coaching Habit* the Foundation Question helps the client to focus on what they want to achieve and not on the coach giving advice.
  - In *Helping people change* the approach is not about giving advice but involves the coach focusing on what the client has already done well and

how they can become more resourceful and resilient when they are in challenging situations.

- In *Third Wave Cognitive Behavioural Coaching* the wide range of therapeutic approaches to facilitate client development are outlined.

- Coaching uses client-generated non-pathological problem descriptions.

  - In *Solution-Focused Coaching* the focus is not on diagnosis but on how the client defines their own problems.
  - In *The Coaching Habit* the AWE Question ensures it is the client's interpretation of their own problem that is paramount.
  - *Helping people change* involves the client deciding on their own interpretation about their challenges and the coach supporting them to achieve their full potential.
  - In *Third Wave Cognitive Behavioural Coaching* the focus is on the range of therapeutic options not on pathological problem descriptions.

- The coach employs a future focus.

  - In *Solution-Focused Coaching* this emphasis is seen from the focus on the client's preferred future.
  - In *The Coaching Habit* the Foundation Question focuses on what the client wants to achieve in the future.
  - In *Helping people change* the emphasis is on the Ideal Self that is clearly future-focused.
  - In *Third Wave Cognitive Behavioural Coaching* the focus is on the therapeutic techniques that can generate a better future for clients.

- The coach strongly believes that positive change will occur.

  - In *Solution-Focused Coaching* this emphasis is seen from the very outset when the coach asks the client what they want to achieve during coaching.
  - In *The Coaching Habit* the Strategic Question focuses on what important positive change the client wants to make.
  - In *Helping people change* the focus on positive emotional activation is central to the approach of positive change.
  - In *Third Wave Cognitive Behavioural Coaching* this is a key under-lying assumption seen in all the therapeutic approaches.

These three books can be seen to have much in common and to demon-strate the core themes of coaching.

Case study: coaching themes

This case study is designed to illustrate the common themes in coaching as set out above.

The focus of coaching is on solutions not problems.

Arin was a warm, smiling, senior executive who worked for a large manufacturing company. After the initial introduction and discussions about confidentiality the coach asked Arin what he wanted to work on and develop. Arin said he needed to improve his assertiveness as he felt that in several situations at work, he ended up backing down over issues and greatly disliking his passivity. This beginning to the coaching illustrates the focus on solutions not problems. The coach could have asked Arin how he was feeling or when the problem started or why he was not as assertive as he wanted but because the coach was solution-focused the process started with asking what the client wanted to work on and develop.

The coach ensures a future focus.

The coach then asked Arin if he woke up tomorrow morning and by some miracle he had become perfectly assertive – what would he be doing differently. This question illustrates how the coach was helping to facilitate Arin's future development and not on understanding the origin of the problem. So, the coach had helped facilitate the development of the client rather than to give advice or to understand the origin of the problem.

The coach helps to facilitate the development capability of the client rather than to give advice.

At this point the coach could easily have gone into teacher mode and talked about the difference between passivity and assertiveness, then gone on to give advice or to teach assertiveness skills. But this is coaching, so the coach listened to Arin talk about how, if he was assertive, he would speak up at meetings, express his point of view loudly and clearly, and repeat himself if needed. The coach asked Arin which of his monthly meeting was easiest for him to speak up in and Aron replied that it was the update meeting that took place on Monday mornings. 'How confident are you that in this meeting you can express your point of view loudly and clearly and repeat yourself if needed?' Arin said that in this meeting he thought he could do this. The two agreed that this action would be homework for Arin who would undertake it before the next coaching session.

Coaching uses client-generated not pathological problem descriptions.

The conversation then moved to Arin talking about his past when he had been told that he had a 'passive personality disorder' by a friend. Arin had been horrified at the amateur diagnosis! The coach listened attentively but then drew the conversation back to what Arin wanted, moving forward. He asked, 'In one year's time, if we were to meet again, what progress would you like to report to me?' This question moved the client from the pathological problem diagnosis of passive personality disorder on to a future focus. Arin said he wanted to never feel disappointment and even disgust at his own passivity.

The coach strongly believes that positive change will occur.

The coach suggested that this was a great direction of travel but that an intermediate level goal may be a great start. Arin suggested that a good short-term goal was to speak up in each of the update meetings that took place on Monday mornings. Arin and the coach agreed to meet in four weeks' time and discuss his progress in being more assertive in the four Monday meetings. As Arin left the session the coach said, 'You know Arin, I think you are going to make excellent progress as I can see you are really committed to being more assertive. Well done!' Arin smiled and said, 'I think you are right!' The coach is clearly expressing his strong belief that positive change will occur.

Reflective practice exercise: Assess your coaching

Think about any recent coaching session and write few sentences about it below.

Example: I had a useful session today with a new CEO who was struggling to build better relationships with her team.

The focus of coaching is on solutions not problems. How much of your session did you spend discussing solutions versus time spent discussing problems?

Example: The client was very talkative and spent more of her time talking about problems.

The coach ensures a future focus. How much of your session did you spend discussing the future versus time spent discussing the past?

Example: Because the client talked so much a lot of time was spent going over the past.

Coaching uses client-generated not pathological problem descriptions. How were problems described in your session?

Example: The problem descriptions were entirely in the client's own words.

The coach strongly believes that positive change will occur. Did you make this clear to your client?

Example: I felt that I could have emphasised this more.

What did you learn by doing this reflective exercise?

Example: I am keen to build understanding and empathy with the client, but perhaps I spend too much time doing this when the client has come to coaching to make progress and move forward.

What are your learnings from the exercise that you can now start to implement in your own practice?

> Example: It is so useful to take the time to consider and reflect on my coaching sessions in a structured way rather than just moving from one client to the next.

Key learning points

1   Coaching is a rapidly growing profession that offers a wide range of assistance to a great variety of individuals.
2   Coaching is a collaborative solution-focused process in which the coach helps clients to enhance their life and reach their personal and professional goals. The more recent use of therapeutic approaches has broadened the reach of coaching.
3   There are many different approaches to coaching and a wide range of books written about the topic. However, the common ideas in many coaching books include: a focus on solutions, not problems, the coach does not give advice but helps facilitate the development capability of the client, the process is future-focused, the coach firmly believes that positive change will occur and coaching uses client-generated not pathological problem descriptions.

Discussion topics

What is the best book on coaching that you have ever read and why was it so good?

Discuss your coaching approach and how well you focus on: solutions, not problems; not giving advice; emphasising the future; expressing the view that positive change is inevitable; and finally using client-generated problem descriptions.

Coaching now has access to a wide range of therapeutic options available to use. Consider a range of these options and decide which ones are the best starting points for you to learn about, experience and apply in your coaching practice.

Suggested readings

Boyatzis, R., Smith, M. L. & Van Oosten, E. (2019). *Helping people change: Coaching with compassion for lifelong learning and growth*. Harvard Business Press.

Passmore, J. & Leach, S. (2022). *Third wave cognitive behavioural coaching: contextual, behavioural and neuroscience approaches for evidence based coaches*. Pavilion Publishing and Media.

Stanier, M. B. (2016). *The coaching habit: Say less, ask more & change the way you lead forever*. Box of Crayons Press.

Szabó, P. & Meier, D. (2009). *Coaching Plain and Simple: Soution-Focused Brief Coaching Essentials*. W.W. Norton & Company.

Chapter 2

Using therapeutic tools in coaching

This chapter explores the background and the long standing use of therapeutic techniques in coaching. It examines the differences between therapy and coaching which include therapy focusing more on the past and coaching more on the future, coaching typically taking place with higher functioning clients than therapy and coaching being focused more on work performance with therapy focusing more on well-being. The chapter provides an examination of the critical importance of ethics when coaches use therapeutic techniques and makes recommendations on when coaches should refer on to other specialists. It also includes an illustrative case study, a reflective practice exercise, key learning points, discussion topics and suggested further reading.

A rich history of the use of therapeutic tools

Coaches have been using therapeutic techniques in their sessions for several decades with the 'grandfather' of coaching Tony Grant writing about this in 2001 (Grant, 2001). In this paper Grant argues that coaching aims to improve both the client's performance at work and in their personal life. He outlines a model of coaching that is based on a combination of cognitive-behavioural therapy and solution-focused therapy suggesting that this approach can form the basis for a psychology of coaching.

By 2011 *The Complete Handbook of Coaching* (Cox, Bachkirova & Clutterbuck, 2011) dedicated 13 chapters to the use of therapeutic techniques in coaching. Included were chapters on the psychodynamic, cognitive behavioural, solution-focused, person centred, gestalt, existential, ontological, narrative, cognitive developmental, transpersonal, positive psychology, transactional analysis and neurolinguistic programme therapeutic approaches.

More recently, as seen in Chapter 1, the book *Third wave cognitive behavioural coaching: contextual, behavioural and neuroscience approaches for evidence based coaches*, edited by Jonathan Passmore and Sarah Leach (Passmore & Leach, 2022), has been produced outlining ten different therapeutic approaches that suitably trained, supervised and ethically adherent coaches can use.

DOI: 10.4324/9781003501824-2

The difference between coaching and therapy

While coaches have used therapeutic techniques in their sessions for many years there are significant differences between coaching and therapy which are summarised below (adapted from Maxwell, 2009).

1   Coaching usually focuses on the present and future, while therapy more often focuses on the past.
2   Coaching takes place with high functioning individuals while therapy is for people with a more severe level of dysfunction or disorder.
3   Coaching is more focused on performance and business improvement while therapy focuses more on individual well-being and recovery.
4   Coaching focuses on understanding personal and business drivers, values and dynamics, while therapy addresses issues at a deeper psychological and emotional level.
5   Therapists are usually highly trained and belong to professional bodies regulated by codes of ethics, formal professional development standards and with disciplinary bodies. Coaches vary greatly in terms of their level of training, but often they belong to professional bodies that have formal ethical standards.
6   Therapists typically charge moderate hourly rates for their services while coaches, particularly executive coaches, often charge much higher rates.

Despite these differences, there are coaches who have formal clinical psychology or other therapeutic qualifications and have adapted therapeutic models for use with high functioning individuals in the workplace. It seems likely that there are also untrained coaches offering therapeutic services to high-functioning individuals, as well as those from the clinical population.

Despite the possibility of unethical practice occurring there are few newspaper or other reports of failed therapy or counselling. However, there are newspaper reports of poorly trained business coaches or misleading coaching business franchises offered as wealth-creation opportunities. There are also arguments that psychologists have neglected the poor and the minorities and focused on the wealthy, but this is rather a different issue (Walker, 2004). Despite this, most professional coaching bodies clearly state the need for coaches to remain within the limits of their trained competence and not to operate in areas where they are unprepared, untrained or unsupervised (Grant, 2006). The mechanics for doing this are not simple as coaches typically define their own limits of practice. This raises the critical issue of ethics in coaching which will be addressed later in the chapter.

The evidence for the use of therapeutic techniques

As this book advocates the use of therapeutic techniques in coaching, below are a sample of the many studies that have been undertaken demonstrating the value of these therapeutic approaches.

Table 2.1 Effectiveness of the use of therapeutic techniques in coaching

Authors	Summary
Gyllensten & Palmer, (2005)	This early study involved 31 British finance-organisation workers using quasi-experimental method and found that anxiety and stress levels initially decreased more in a coaching group than in the control group and that the effects were maintained at the end of the study. However, this result was not replicated with depression levels.
Green, Oades & Grant, (2006)	This paper examined the effects of a ten-week cognitive-behavioural, solution-focused life coaching group programme on a group of 28 coaching participants and 28 waitlist control members and showed the coaching produced significant increases in goal striving, well-being and hope, with some gains maintained for 30 weeks.
Kearns, Forbes & Gardiner, (2007)	This study examined the efficacy of a six-week cognitive behavioural coaching programme, in reducing levels of perfectionism and self-handicapping in 28 higher-degree students and found that during the workshop levels of perfectionism fell and this was sustained at follow-up, while levels of self-handicapping didn't fall during the workshop but by the follow up had done so significantly. The authors concluded that cognitive behavioural coaching can be successfully used with a nonclinical population.
Gardiner, Kearns, & Tiggemann (2013)	The study assessed the relationship between cognitive behavioural coaching and the well-being of rural general practitioners, their intentions to leave and their actual leaving general practice. The coaching produced lower distress scores and over a three-year period, 94 per cent of the coaching group remained in general practice compared with 80 per cent of the control group.
Prevatt, & Yelland (2015)	This study evaluated an eight-week ADHD coaching programme in 148 college students and showed significant improvement in ten areas of study and learning strategies, symptom distress and greater satisfaction with school and work and on self-esteem. The results were consistent across different semesters, time of semester, and different novice coaches.
Curtis & O'Beso (2017)	This article investigated the efficacy of a telephone pain management coaching programme in improving outcomes for adults with chronic pain. There was a significant reduction in the pain scores from intake to six- and 12-months follow-up, and the findings support the implementation of pain management coaching as an effective adjunctive intervention.
Grant (2017)	This book presents a summary of research into the use of solution-focused cognitive–behavioural coaching into performance, stress, and resilience. The overview indication is that workplace coaching can be effective in assisting people deal with stress, fatigue and burnout.

Authors	Summary
Skews (2018)	This randomised controlled trial study into the efficacy a brief Acceptance and Commitment Therapy coaching used 65 coached and 65 waitlist control participants and found significant increases for the coached subjects in life satisfaction, general mental health, self-efficacy, situational intrinsic motivation, goal-directed thinking, goal attainment, and psychological flexibility.
Levin et al. (2019)	This study examined app-based skill coaching from 39 non-clinical adults in a randomized controlled trial using Acceptance and Commitment Coaching. Overall, the results suggest that this ACT (Acceptance and Commitment Training) app coaching can have immediate, positive impact on psychological functioning.
Lungu et al. (2021)	This study was used to test the efficacy of real-world, structured, cognitive behavioural coaching delivered via video or telephone, which concluded that this is a promising approach that could significantly increase access to affordable coaching for emotional health care.
Tomoiagă & David (2023)	A systematic review to investigate 26 quantitative studies in Cognitive Behavioural Coaching which showed that it had a moderate positive impact with high level improvements in performance and low to medium improvements on abilities, affect, and cognition.

The importance of ethics in using therapeutic techniques

As this book is about presenting therapeutic techniques for use by coaches, there are many important ethical issues which include the following, summarised from Brennan and Wildflower (2010).

1 Competence: Is the coach thoroughly trained in their areas of practice? Has the training been with a reliable training organisation? Does the coach have regular documented supervision with a fully qualified individual? Does the coach undertake regular formal self-reflection?

2 Limits: Does the coach know their limits of competence; do they remain within them and do they refer clients on to other professionals when they encounter issues outside the area of their competence?

3 Consent: Does the coach have a structured process to gain written or verbal agreement from the client to undertake coaching? Has the coach explained the nature and process of coaching sufficiently clearly, so the client is able to make an informed consent?

4 Integration: Has the coach explained the nature of the therapeutic intervention and how it fits with the overall coaching process and goals?

5 Confidentiality: Has the coach explained the nature of confidentiality and has the client agreed to this? What confidentiality agreement has been reached? If the coaching is being paid for by an organisation, what information does it have access to?

6   Misrepresentation: Has the coach been honest, frank and direct in how they described their experience, qualifications and capability?
7   Bias: Does the coach know their own biases and prejudices, and what has been done to counter these?

The Ethical Eight

The practical steps a coach should undertake before using therapeutic techniques with a client include undertaking:

1   Formal training in coaching with a reputable coaching organisation that uses an evidence-based approach. This may be from universities such as Henley Business School, the University of East London, the University of Sydney in Australia or the Coach Certificate Program at the Weatherhead School of Management Case Western University in the USA. Training may also be from organisations accredited with bodies such as EMCC Global and the International Coaching Federation.
2   Coaches should have undertaken coaching for themselves to deal with their own personal issues so they understand the process from the client's perspective and so they can build their own self-awareness.
3   They should have undertaken formal training in the evidence-based therapeutic approach.
4   Coaches should have therapy for themselves using the relevant therapeutic approach, so they have an experiential understanding of it.
5   They should have professional/ethical/cultural safety training and adherence relevant to such issues as the limits of competence, consent, confidentiality, misrepresentation and personal bias. This usually takes place by joining and practicing the standards as set out by the profession's institution.
6   Coaches should undertake screening for high functioning clients as part of case conceptualisation to ensure that they are not unknowingly dealing with more deeply disturbed clients.
7   They need ongoing, regular, documented supervision with a senior well-trained professional.
8   Coaches should have reflective-practice-based professional development so that they can be confident that they are staying up to date and fully competent within their scope of practice.

It is vital that coaches also only use psychotherapeutic techniques after considering the existing evidence of their relevance, applicability and effectiveness.

Who to coach and who not to

Tony Grant in the definition of coaching used earlier in the chapter talked about coaches working with normal, non-clinical clients. A common term for this group is high functioning clients – but what does this mean? The Cambridge Dictionary (2023) indicates that high functioning means working very effectively and successfully.

Non-clinical high functioning clients are those that share three basic characteristics: psychological, social and career stability.

- Psychological stability means the person is usually able to regulate their emotional and cognitive states to a sufficient extent to achieve their personal goals including a sense of well-being.
- Social stability means being able to maintain a range of different relationships both professional, friendship and intimate to achieve a sense of fulfilment in life.
- Vocational stability means the person can hold down a regular job despite the inevitable upsets and problems of life.

Carl Rogers, the humanistic psychologist, said that the fully functioning person is someone who has accepted "existential living". That is, they can live fully in the present moment and experience their inner freedom, creativity, excitement, and challenge. These individuals are aware of their own feelings and reactions but are not controlled by them. They are also flexible, constantly take in new information and experiences and embrace change and learning (Rogers, 1962).

Fully functioning individuals tend to have certain positive characteristics that enable them to understand their own emotions and grow personally and professionally (Cherry, 2002). Some of these characteristics include:

- Accepting reality and not needing to deny or distort experiences
- Being able to change based on their experience and insights
- Being un-defensive about experiences or comments
- Living harmoniously with other people
- Being open to experience
- Being open to feedback and being willing to change when needed
- Being able to trust one's own judgement and experiences
- Having an unconditional self-regard for themselves and others

A Harvard Graduate School of Education professor of adult learning, Robert Kegan, suggests that as we grow, we move through a series of levels of development during our lives (Kegan, 1982). The higher three levels of functioning include:

- At stage 3, people have grown to the point where they can see themselves as part of something larger, e.g., a family, a community, a nation, but often are unable to resolve conflicting viewpoints with others.

- At stage 4 people can own their own work, make their own decisions and can be internally motivated. They can see different points of view but are driven by their own values.
- At stage 5, people can see both their own and others' points of view and see an issue from multiple perspectives.

This notion of high-functioning clients is important because coaches are not usually trained or competent to deal with clinical clients. This latter group consists of people who have behavioural and mental health issues that significantly disrupt their ability to cope (Wikipedia, 2024b) including:

- Traumatic stress reactions
- Significant emotional and psychological problems, including serious mental illness
- Severe interpersonal or social problems and dysfunctions
- Behavioural problems including significant substance abuse and dependence
- Serious intellectual, cognitive, and neurological conditions

The limits of professional competence and referral on

It is vital that coaches know and work within their scope of practice – that is the areas in which they have been fully trained and supervised. When coaches get close to the boundaries of their competence they need to refer on. If the coach feels uncomfortable or unclear about an important issue they should talk to their client about the limits of their training and ability and discuss the idea of a referral to a specialist in the area. This topic should also be discussed openly between the coach and their supervisor. The International Coaching Federation have a useful publication called *Referring a client to therapy: a set of guidelines* (ICF, 2024) which is summarised below.

Cues for referring a client on, include when:

- The coach feels anxious, stressed or uncomfortable about a topic the client is working on.
- The client asks for help in an area where the coach has little or no expertise.
- The client is becoming dependent on the coach, for example, repeatedly asking for direct guidance, frequent phone calls, emails or texts outside of the coaching session, extravagant praise for the coach and the need to contact the coach before making minor decisions.
- The coach feels that they can no longer offer the client assistance and begin to feel that they are failing.
- The coach feels responsible beyond the normal professional boundaries.

Coaches should also refer on when the challenges start to interfere with the client's ability to take care of themselves from a health care, vocational, social or psychological perspective.

The following are some of the signs that a referral is necessary:

- Anxiety that begins to disrupt the client's self-care
- Eating disorders where the client feels they lack control
- Persistent sadness or self-loathing or signs of depression
- Major mood changes including anger, frustration, worry or guilt
- Substance abuse or signs of addiction
- Flashbacks or other signs of post-traumatic disturbance
- Thoughts of self-harm or suicide
- Dissociative disorders which include feelings of a loss of connection between the individual and their identity
- A significantly decreased ability to cope at work or home

As part of the development of every coach, they should make initial contact with a clinical psychologist or other specialist health professional and be able to refer on comfortably with this individual. The ability to refer on to another professional is vital for both client care and for the confidence of the coach (ICF, 2024).

Case study: coaching competence

Brian had been an accountant for 12 years with a major professional services firm. He spent his time in the audit department initially as an auditor, then as a team leader then as staff partner. He had come to a point where he enjoyed his people development role more than supervising technical audit work. After 12 years he decided he wanted a change and undertook a coaching training programme. This involved 100 coach-specific training hours and consisted of a mix of online classes and independent learning. He regularly attended supervision once he started to undertake pro bono client work. He found the work extremely interesting and fulfilling. After completing the qualification, he approached several accounting firms and was able to rapidly obtain work coaching first line managers. His background in the profession was very helpful and enabled him to understand the pressures and challenges that his clients had. He joined the European Mentoring and Coaching Council (EMCC) which provided coaching professional accreditation, as well as support and guidance. After about a year of working in this way he decided he wanted to extend his skills and enrolled in a cognitive behavioural therapy course for coaches. This enabled him to start to better identify unhelpful thinking patterns in his clients and to help then to change these patterns. At this stage, he had an experienced executive coach as his supervisor but also decided to engage a clinical psychologist as a specialist supervisor in the cognitive behavioural area. He also had a series of eight sessions with the clinical psychologist to work on some of his own residual imposter phenomenon issues and found this approach to be very helpful. After three years as a coach Brian felt satisfied that he was competent to deal with professional service firm clients and to assist then by using cognitive behavioural techniques.

Reflective practice exercise: ethics

Consider each of the following ethical issues.

Have you had formal training in coaching with a reputable coaching organisation that uses an evidence-based approach?

Example: Yes, I have undertaken a Masters in Coaching Psychology.

Have you undertaking coaching for yourself so that you understand the process from the client's perspective?

Example: Yes, I have had 12 sessions with an experienced coach to help me understand what it is like to walk in the client's shoes.

If you use any therapeutic techniques, have you had training in that evidence-based therapeutic approach?

Example: Yes, I went to a one week compassion-based counselling course to learn about this area.

If you use any therapeutic technique, have you worked with a relevant professional on your own issues or challenges using this therapeutic approach?

Example: Yes, I have spent time with a compassion-based therapist.

Have you had training in relevant professional/ethical/cultural safety issues and do you adhere to a code of professional ethics?

Example: Yes, I belong to EMCC and follow their code of ethics.

Do you routinely screen clients to assess their level of functioning as part of case conceptualisation and do you ensure that you are not unknowingly dealing with more deeply disturbed clients?

Example: Yes, I regularly assess clients' psychological, social and vocational stability, and I would refer on if necessary.

Do you have ongoing, regular, documented supervision with a senior well-trained professional?

Example: Yes, I use Dr Mary Holland as a supervisor and find these sessions very helpful.

Do you undertake regular reflective-practice-based professional development and stay up to date and fully competent within your scope of practice.

Example: Yes, I undertake regular professional development with EMCC.

Key learning points

1   Coaching has a rich history of using evidence-based therapeutic techniques including psychodynamic, cognitive behavioural, solution-focused, person centred, gestalt, existential, ontological, narrative, cognitive developmental, transpersonal, positive psychology, transactional analysis and neurolinguistic programme approaches.
2   Coaching provides services to the high functioning normal population which include people with a significant degree of psychological, social and vocational stability. This is contrasted with the clinical population which includes individuals with more complex and severe challenges.
3   Coaching differs from therapy in a range of ways including the focus that coaching has on the present and future while therapy more often focuses on the past.
4   Coaches using therapeutic techniques need to be fully trained, supervised and ethically adherent. The Ethical Eight is a simple list of the requirements that coaches should complete if they are to use therapeutic techniques.
5   Coaches need to have a clear understanding of the limits of their professional competence and refer on to specialists when they are close to the limits of their training and expertise.

Discussion topics

Consider the types of ethical issue you have seen in your practice. How do you deal with these issues?

What is the difference between the clinical and the coaching population? What questions are critical to ask clients to determine which population they belong to?

If a coach has learned about a therapeutic approach such as Acceptance and Commitment Therapy but has not undertaken any therapy or coaching themselves using this approach, should they use it in their practice?

Suggested Reading

Hill, J. & Oliver, J. (2018). *Acceptance and commitment coaching: Distinctive features.* Routledge.

Neenan, M. & Dryden, W. (2020). *Cognitive Behavioural Coaching: A Guide to Problem Solving and Personal Development.* Routledge.

Neenan, M. & Palmer, S. (Eds). (2021). *Cognitive behavioural coaching in practice: An evidence based approach.* Routledge.

Chapter 3

The schema coaching approach

This chapter begins with an exploration of the evolution of coaching through the first, second and third waves and introduces the schema approach. It reviews a sample of the effectiveness literature on schema therapy. The chapter outlines the list of early maladaptive and then the positive schema that are typically seen in coaching. It then sets out the types of challenges the coaches typically see in their work with clients and outlines the way in which the schema approach can help coaches develop a deep understanding of them. It also includes an illustrative case study, a reflective practice exercise, key learning points, discussion topics and suggested further reading.

First-, second- and third-wave coaching

Coaching has developed through a series of waves that have reflected the advances in the psychology of human learning. First-wave cognitive behavioural coaching aided the initial development of coaching and then formed the basis of the subsequent second- and third-wave frameworks.

First-wave or behavioural coaching started from the work of John B. Watson, Edward Thorndike and Ivan Pavlov with their research in the early part of the 20th century. These pioneers examined learning through the association or pairing of stimulus and response in what was called classical conditioning. Subsequently learning theory focused more on the work of B. F. Skinner and the use of rewards and punishment called operant conditioning to shape behaviour. Finally learning theory drew on the work of Albert Bandura and the impact of social learning which argued that observation and imitation were also critical to learning (Leach, 2022).

Second-wave cognitive behavioural approaches were developed in the 1960s and were influenced by the work of researchers into the development of thinking and language. Cognitive therapy was initially developed by an American psychologist, Albert Ellis, and called rational emotive therapy. Ellis believed that distressed individuals often developed self-defeating thoughts based on their irrational core beliefs. He found that challenging these beliefs and thoughts through rational analysis assisted clients in finding resolution to their distress. Another early pioneer, Arron Beck, developed cognitive therapy based on the idea that client's perception, interpretation and attribution of meaning to events

DOI: 10.4324/9781003501824-3

was what caused them distress but also provided them with a path out of this. Cognitive therapy suggested that the awareness and challenging of unhelpful thinking was particularly important in providing clients with a new way of dealing with environmental triggers that caused distress (Passmore & Leach, 2022).

Third-wave cognitive behavioural coaching was typically based on more complex approaches such as that seen in acceptance and commitment therapy, schema therapy, cognitive based therapy and dialectical behaviour therapy. These approaches have in common:

- The importance of the relationship between the client's thinking, emotion and behaviour
- The significance of the client's personal core values and identity
- The value of being able to identify and choose which thoughts and emotions to act upon
- A strong base of evidence which demonstrates their efficacy

(Passmore & Leach, 2022)

Schema coaching

Schema coaching, derived from schema therapy, is an example of a third-wave approach. Schema therapy was originally developed by the American psychologist Jeffery E. Young and colleagues in the early 2000s to treat clients with personality and other chronic psychological disorders (Young et al., 2003). Young felt that many therapies had helpful approaches but that by themselves these were often not enough to help clients with chronic persistent disorders. Schema therapy is different from many other therapies as it combines and integrates approaches from psychodynamic therapy, behaviour therapy, cognitive behavioural therapy, gestalt therapy and attachment theory. An early maladaptive schema is a cluster of feelings, thoughts and behaviour that is persistent and dysfunctional. Schema often develop early and can impact the client throughout the course of their lifetime. For example, an individual with a failure schema may have achieved a great deal in their life, but still believe that they will fail at any time.

Some 20 years after the work of Young, McCormick (2022) developed schema coaching by utilising the schema therapy approach and adapting it for leaders, executives and others in the workplace. The schema approach may have relevance outside the workplace. However, this has yet to be explored in detail. Like schema therapy, schema coaching aims to help clients address long-standing persistent challenges and to build adaptive thoughts, feelings and behaviours.

The effectiveness of schema therapy and coaching

Schema coaching is a recent development (McCormick, 2022) and so at this stage very little effectiveness research has been undertaken on it and so the supporting evidence on the effectiveness of schema therapy is presented below. The table has been adapted from McCormick (2022).

Table 3.1 Sample of schema therapy efficacy research studies

Study	Summary
Nordahl & Nysaeter (2005)	The authors analysed results from a single case series trial of six borderline personality disorder patients who undertook schema therapy. They found that improvements from baseline to follow-up were large, and these were clinically meaningful for five of the six patients.
Giesen-Bloo et al. (2006)	The authors conducted a random controlled trial comparing schema therapy to transference-focused psychotherapy in 86 patients over a period of three years and a one-year follow-up. They found both therapies effective in reducing borderline personality disorder and general psychiatric symptoms while improving the quality of life. Of the two therapies schema was the most effective.
Farrell et al. (2009)	This study compared the effectiveness of group schema therapy with 32 borderline personality disorder outpatients where it was given in addition to treatment as usual, with a control group of 16 patients that received only treatment as usual. Dropout rates from schema therapy were zero compared with 25 per cent for treatment as usual. Schema therapy produced significant reductions in both borderline personality disorder and other psychiatric symptoms, with large effect sizes.
Nadort et al. (2009)	The study used a random controlled design and compared individualised schema therapy with telephone crisis support provided by the therapist. They found that after one and a half years of schema therapy 42 per cent of the patients had recovered from borderline personality disorder.
Carter et al. (2013)	The authors used a random controlled design and compared schema therapy to cognitive behavioural therapy in the treatment of depression. They found that both therapies were equally effective.
Malogiannis et al. (2014)	The study used a single case series without a control group to examine the effectiveness of schema therapy in treating chronic depression patients. By the end of therapy about 60 per cent of patients had symptoms in remission or had responded satisfactorily.
Bamelis et al. (2014)	The researchers used a multicentre randomised controlled trial of the clinical effectiveness of schema therapy for personality disorders. They found that a significantly greater number of patients recovered in schema therapy group compared with treatment as usual and clarification-oriented psychotherapy.
Dickhaut & Arntz (2014)	The authors conducted a pilot study that used the combination of group and individual schema therapy for patients with borderline personality disorder. They found large improvements on general psychopathological symptoms, schema mode measures, quality of life, and happiness with these patients.

Study	Summary
Renner et al. (2013)	This article described how schema therapy was adapted and used to treat chronic depression. The authors concluded that schema therapy appeared to be a promising treatment approach for depression which targeted important underlying risk factors.
Reiss et al. (2014)	This paper reported on the results of three pilot studies of inpatient schema therapy with patients suffering from severe borderline personality disorder. Results showed that inpatient schema therapy significantly reduced symptoms of severe borderline personality disorder and global severity of psychopathology.
Videler et al. (2014)	The authors used a one group pre/post design to investigate the effects of schema group therapy in older outpatients. Short-term group schema cognitive behaviour therapy resulted in significant improvements in all three measures of psychological symptoms, early maladaptive schema and modes with medium effect sizes.
Peeters, van Passel & Krans (2022)	This study is a systematic review of the effectiveness of schema therapy for patients with anxiety disorders, obsessive compulsive disorder and post-traumatic stress disorder. The results showed that schema therapy led to positive effects in these disorders and in early maladaptive schemas.
Kopf-Beck et al. (2024)	The authors used a randomized clinical trial to compare the effectiveness of schema therapy, cognitive behavioural therapy and individual supportive therapy for depression in inpatient and day clinic settings. They found that all therapy types were effective and that schema therapy was a potentially useful treatment of depression.
Mansourzadeh et al. (2024)	This study used a random controlled trial to examine the effectiveness of schema therapy on anxiety, depression, fatigue, quality of life, and sleep in patients with multiple sclerosis. They found that there was a significant decrease in anxiety and depression in the schema therapy group compared with the control group.
Kalantarian et al. (2024)	The authors studied the effects of schema therapy and dialectical behaviour therapy on cognitive emotion regulation in patients with bipolar disorder. They found that both therapy types improved emotional self-regulation in these patients.

Schema analysis

Schema coaching uses three levels of analysis to help build a comprehensive understanding of the client. These levels are early schemas, coping styles and modes which can be defined as follows:

1   The early maladaptive and adaptive or positive schemas are enduring patterns of feelings, thoughts and behaviours.
2   The coping mechanisms are ways that clients try in vain to control, eliminate or reduce the schema pain and frustration.
3   The schema modes or mood state changes which are moment by moment responses to everyday issues.

The original early maladaptive schema

The original five domains and 18 early maladaptive schema developed by Young and colleagues (Young et al., 2003) and used in schema therapy are summarised below.

First domain: Disconnection/Rejection

1   Abandonment/Instability
2   Mistrust/Abuse
3   Emotional Deprivation
4   Defectiveness/Shame
5   Social Isolation/Alienation

Second domain: Impaired autonomy and or performance

Dependence/Incompetence
Vulnerability to Harm or Illness
Enmeshment/Undeveloped Self
Failure to Achieve

Third domain: Impaired limits

Entitlement/Grandiosity
Insufficient Self-Control/Self-Discipline

Fourth domain: Other directedness

Subjugation
Self-Sacrifice
Approval-Seeking/Recognition-Seeking

Fifth domain: Over-Vigilance/Inhibition

Negativity/Pessimism
Emotional Inhibition
Unrelenting Standards/Hyper-criticalness
Punitiveness

The schema frequently seen in coaching

After using the schema approach for many years with executives and team members in the workplace the following schema were found to be most prevalent in this group of clients.

Unrelenting striving

This overlaps with the Unrelenting Standards/Hyper-criticalness schema developed by Young and is the most common seen in the competitive corporate or professional service environment. With this schema the client is extremely hard working and frequently believes that they must continue at this gruelling pace to meet their own and the organisations very high performance standards. These clients frequently have a savage inner critic that drives them on to achieve more with cruel and continuous condemnation. They find it hard to slow down, have difficulty in not working in the evenings and weekends and often fail to take their annual leave. They can also be harsh critics of others including their leader, their team, their suppliers and customers. Organisational goal setting and individual performance appraisal systems often reinforce this schema with their endless demands for greater and greater achievement. These clients often sacrifice family time for the sake of work. Colloquially this is often called workaholism or work addiction.

Sense of failure

This overlaps with Young's Failure to Achieve schema and is commonly seen in executives who have done very well or been promoted rapidly or at a pace they did not expect. They believe that despite their achievements in life, that they have failed, will fail, or that they are not as good or worthy as their peers. These clients often have a very persistent inner critic that is telling them that any success is just luck, one-off or temporary. The frequency, immediacy and persuasiveness of the inner critic is a characteristic of these clients. They find it hard to accept complements or recognition and will sometimes not try for promotion because of their sense of impending failure. They often end up achieving well below their potential and spending excessive amounts of time and energy worrying about possible public humiliation or other failure. Colloquially this is often called imposter syndrome, impostor phenomenon or impostorism.

Needing approval

This overlaps with Young's Approval-seeking/Recognition-seeking schema and is commonly seen in executives with a sense of inadequacy or personal shortcoming and who despite their achievements, have a strong belief that they need too much attention approval or recognition from their manager, peers or team members. Executives who struggle to delegate, overly protect their team members from pressure and too readily accept responsibility for problems outside their control, often suffer from this schema. They frequently say what they think other people want to hear rather than express their views directly. These clients often struggle to make decisions without gaining the views and support of others. In demanding corporate or professional service environments these individuals can become exploited by leaders, team members and customers as they are often too willing to undertake others' tasks or responsibilities. They often need excessive reassurance and suffer from a sense of inadequacy. They are often willing to make personal and family sacrifices to seek approval at work, even if later it generates family or personal resentment. Colloquially these people are often called 'needy souls'.

Self-sacrifice

This overlaps with Young's schema of the same name. It is frequently seen in the health and other caring professions where clients are constantly exposed to individuals with very high and urgent needs. These professionals often feel that their own needs are unimportant and certainly can be delayed because of the intense and critical needs of others. They often rationalise that they are self-sufficient but later can resent the demands of the job and the clientele. Their individual and social identity is often their role or profession – they feel they are their job and have little of value outside work. They gain a strong sense of identity but typically fail to have their own needs met. They will often work very long hours, skip meals, exercise or relaxation to meet the needs of their leaders, team members or customers. They are typically very sensitive to the difficulties, pain or needs of others and feel a compelling need to address these, at their own cost.

Lack of support

This overlaps with Young's Abandonment schema and the Emotional Deprivation schema. It is often seen in competitive organisations where corrosive politics and betrayal are evident. The client has the belief that despite what they have already achieved in life that significant others have not supported them enough, financially, emotionally or career wise. This is seen in executives who feel that at any time their CEO or board chair will openly criticise them or not protect them from the unfair criticism of others. Paradoxically, these individuals often work in organisations which are by their very nature insecure, for example research groups that are totally dependent on external grants or commercial entities with only one customer. This commercial insecurity can be used to justify their own personal insecurity and sense of abandonment during challenging times.

Excessive involvement with others

This overlaps with Young's Enmeshment/Undeveloped self schema and is seen with clients who have an overly strong connection with a significant other such as a parent, teacher, leader or spouse. This connection means that the individual has little room to develop their own sense of self and is unsure of their own wants, desires, needs and values. In the workplace these clients can become very dependent on their manager or a peer for support and need their constant input or acknowledgement. They may feel unclear about their capabilities and their career direction.

Pessimism

This overlaps with Young's Negativity/Pessimism schema and is seen with clients who feel that they dwell too much on the betrayal, disappointments, losses, conflicts and failures of the past. They tend to minimise or trivialise the positive aspects of life. They often work in areas which reinforce their pessimism about life such as prison officers, police, population obesity researchers or related areas. They often fail to achieve their career potential because their organisations believe that they lack positivity and drive. These clients can often suffer from productivity challenges as they spend a great deal of time and energy on problems that they cannot control or even influence. They can end up lonely as friends drift away unable to deal with the pessimism.

Lack of spontaneity

This overlaps with Young's Emotional Inhibition schema. It is seen in workers who feel that they must control, contain and suppress their natural spontaneous actions, communications or feelings because others may not approve or because they may not be able to control their expression once it starts. This is seen in team members who work in a benign culture but who feel unable to express their frustration, disappointment, enthusiasm or vulnerability. This is also seen in professional service firms that have a strongly rational, rules-driven, legislative-focused atmosphere for example, accountants and lawyers. The individuals often express feelings of being 'up tight' and 'suppressed' yet are unable to understand why. They typically are living in a way that conflicts with their impulses and choose a controlling culture to help with their perceived need for control. They often stop themselves from gaining enjoyment out of spontaneity and naturalness.

Feeling controlled

This overlaps with Young's subjugation schema. Despite having achieved a lot in their lives and careers these people often give up control of important areas to others. They frequently relinquish control because the dominant figure is 'always right' or 'must be obeyed'. This means that their own needs do not get met. However, they do avoid the criticism or disapproval of the other person. They feel that their views are not important even when they are actually correct. They are often very compliant and can end up in jobs with very dominating leaders. In the longer term these clients frequently feel trapped and can become passive aggressive or dependent on alcohol or other drugs. An example may be a professional with a large mortgage working for a deeply insensitive boss feeling trapped, unfulfilled but unwilling to change jobs.

Why we see fewer maladaptive schema in coaching

To contrast the early maladaptive schema developed by Young and colleagues (Young et al., 2003) and those typically seen in the coaching population, both lists are set out below.

Schema seen in therapy

1 Abandonment/Instability
2 Mistrust/Abuse
3 Emotional Deprivation
4 Defectiveness/Shame
5 Social Alienation/Rejection
6 Dependence/Incompetence
7 Vulnerability to Harm/Illness
8 Enmeshment/Undeveloped Self
9 Failure
10 Entitlement/Grandiosity
11 Insufficient Self-Control/Self-Discipline
12 Subjugation
13 Self-Sacrifice
14 Approval-Seeking/Recognition-Seeking
15 Negativity/Pessimism
16 Emotional Inhibition
17 Unrelenting Standards/Hyper-criticalness
18 Punitiveness

Schema often seen in coaching

1 Unrelenting striving
2 Sense of failure
3 Needing approval
4 Self-sacrifice
5 Lack of support

6   Excessive involvement with others
7   Pessimism
8   Lack of spontaneity
9   Feeling controlled.

As can be seen above, there are many more early maladaptive schemas seen in therapy than in coaching. This is a result of the different populations seen in therapy as compared with coaching. In Chapter 2 coaching was said to involve working with the high functioning, normal, non-clinical population that share three basic characteristics: psychological, social and career stability. This results in individuals with fewer schema for example in the impaired autonomy and performance area.

More especially, as coaching clients are typically psychologically stable, they are unlikely to suffer from the Instability or Defectiveness schema. As they are socially stable, they unlikely to be impacted from the Alienation schema. As they have a degree of career stability there are few instances of the Insufficient Self Control schema. More research is needed to confirm these suggestions.

In the clinical population there are more disturbed clients so schema such as Abuse, Emotional deprivation and Insufficient Self-control are more common. Bach and colleagues used a large Danish sample of clinical and nonclinical adults and identified four schema clusters as differentiating the two groups. They called these 1) Disconnection and Rejection; 2) Impaired Autonomy and Performance; 3) Excessive Responsibility and Standards; and 4) Impaired Limits. All four schema clusters differentiated clinical and non-clinical samples in terms of need-thwarting parental experiences (Bach, Lockwood & Young, 2018).

In the prison population there are more individuals with abuse and impaired limits types of schema. This is supported by a study of prisoners in Iran, where Esmat Shojaadini and Yaser Azizi Saeid found that the most common early maladaptive schema were Mistrust/abuse, Defectiveness/shame, Abandonment/instability, Insufficient self-control/self-discipline and Emotional deprivation (Shojaadini & Saeid, 2019).

Bishop et al. (2022) undertook a systematic review and meta-analysis of early maladaptive schema and depression and found that all 18 early maladaptive schemas were positively correlated with depression with the largest effect sizes for Defectiveness/shame and Social isolation.

Riso et al. (2006) assessed the long-term stability of early maladaptive schema in 55 depressed outpatients for up to five years and found they were moderate to highly stable, even after controlling for severity of depression and neuroticism. The results suggest that early maladaptive schema are about as stable as personality disorder features.

In conclusion there are important differences between the types of schema that are seen in therapy and coaching. Clients coming to coaching who are more psychologically, socially and vocationally stable appear to suffer from a smaller set of schema which include what are often less severe disbalances. In the clinical population, early maladaptive schema are relatively stable as suggested by Young et al. (2003).

Positive or adaptive schema

Schema therapy has been developed with a focus on the early maladaptive patterns that have driven clients to therapy. These patterns are a result of not having core emotional needs met. These core childhood needs include secure attachments to others such as safety, stability, nurturance and acceptance, autonomy confidence and sense of identity, freedom to express valid needs and emotions, spontaneity and play, realistic limits and self-control (Young et al., 2003).

Later work in the area proposed that clients not only had early maladaptive schema but also positive schema or early *adaptive* schema. These early adaptive schema are summarised below (Videler, et al., 2020):

1 Emotional fulfilment: the ability to feel content and satisfied with life
2 Success: a feeling of accomplishment and attainment
3 Empathic consideration: the ability to emotionally understand other people, their thoughts and feelings from their point of view
4 Optimism: being able to see the positive side of situations and people
5 Emotional openness and spontaneity: being receptive to new ideas or experiences and being able to react without undue constraint
6 Self-compassion: being able to relate to yourself with forgiveness, acceptance and love
7 Healthy boundaries: being able to set realistic limits on your own and other peoples' communication and behaviour
8 Social belonging: the ability to connect and interact with others in a positive way over a sustained period
9 Healthy self-control: the ability to regulate your thoughts and behaviour in a way that avoids undesirable or unacceptable outcomes
10 Realistic expectations: being able to anticipate outcomes of events that are likely to eventuate
11 Self-directedness: having a sense of self-determination and the ability to regulate and adapt behaviour to meet the demands of a situation
12 Healthy self-interest and self-care: the ability to look after yourself in a way that promotes and maintains health, prevents disease and in a way that does not necessarily need the assistance of others
13 Stable attachment: the ability to maintain positive relationships that are reciprocal
14 Healthy self-reliance/competence: the ability to independently choose and undertake a course of action in a way that achieved the desired goals

John Louis and colleagues reported the psychometric properties of the Young Positive Schema Questionnaire using confirmatory factor analysis (Louis et al., 2018). They identified the following positive schema which are summarised below.

1   Emotional fulfilment and stable attachment: –the belief that the person has someone who will listen and understand, nurture and care deeply about them
2   Empathic consideration: the person feels that they can accept that they do not always have to get their own way in group decisions and can see others perspectives
3   Emotional openness: the person can show their emotions comfortably and feel that important others care about them, are expressive and spontaneous
4   Developed self: the person can establish an independent life and is not overly involved with their parents or care givers and their difficulties. They believe that their parents or care givers are not trying to live vicariously through them
5   Healthy self-control: the person can discipline themselves enough to complete boring tasks and not easily give up.
6   Success: the person believes that they are as talented as most people and usually do as well or better than others
7   Optimism: the person generally feels safe and secure and believes that serious financial problems, illnesses, or catastrophic events are unlikely to happen to them
8   Self-compassion and realistic expectations: the person believes that when they make a mistake, they can generally give themselves the benefit of the doubt, forgive themselves and do not feel that they deserve punishment
9   Social belonging: the person usually fits in and feels included in the groups they mix with

I have found this shorter list of psychometrically sound schema to be helpful in schema coaching.

Coping styles

Individuals develop schema early in life and then typically spend many years learning to cope with these. Humans, like other animals, have three basic responses to danger or threat: fight, flight and freeze. The three basic responses have relevance to the coping styles seen in schema analysis: overcompensation, avoidance and surrender. The three coping styles developed by Young and colleagues are used by clients in the forlorn hope that they will alleviate or eliminate the hurt caused by the maladaptive schemas. These coping styles are:

- Schema surrender: This is seen when clients simply capitulate or give in to the schema. They often feel the struggle against it is hopeless or in many cases have never considered any other response but surrender. For example, a client with the pessimism schema believes that things will inevitably go wrong and so will not invest any time or energy into challenging this idea.
- Schema avoidance: This style is seen when clients try to escape from the impact of the schema. For example, a client with the sense of failure schema may take on a job that is menial so that their likelihood of failure is avoided.
- Schema compensation: This style is seen when clients attempt to do the exact opposite of what the schema would indicate. For example, a client suffering with the pessimism schema may regularly engage in high-risk recreation such as sky diving in defiance of their focus on the negative.

Schema modes

Schema modes are the present moment emotional states and responses both positive and negative that we experience every day. Schema modes are typically caused by the things that happen to us – our emotional triggers. They may be a moment of anger caused by someone misunderstanding us or a moment of rational reassurance that is triggered by a kind friend. Unlike the more stable maladaptive schema, these schema modes or moods change rapidly over time, given the fluctuations in our environment. We may feel excited and pleased to see an old friend but then suddenly realise that this friend was unkind to us during our last encounter. So, we may move rapidly between the feelings of excitement and pleasure to the feelings of frustration and resentment. Schema modes may be defined as the emotional states, survival mechanisms or healthy behaviours that are active and anyone moment for the individual.

In the context of a schema coaching session, we may see that a client with the needing approval schema may be ingratiating and warm at the beginning of the session but suddenly express the anger and resentment at not being able to be recognised by others.

Common types of schema modes summarised from Roediger et al. (2018) include the following:

- Child mode: in which the client expresses primitive and often repressed emotions when their needs are not met. The coach may suddenly see the vulnerable child, abandoned child, the abused child, the deprived child, or the rejected child.
- Inner critic modes: in which the client's internalised core harmful messages, beliefs and judgements play loudly in their head. These can be punitive – 'You know that you are an idiot' or demeaning modes – 'You will fail at this one, for sure'.

- Maladaptive coping modes: in which the client tries to deal with their unhelpful child and inner critic modes in a way that often makes the situation worse. Examples can include compliant surrender (giving in to the schema), detached protector (shutting down or zoning out), detached self-soother (anesthetising using drugs, self-stimulating or other forms of escape), and attack mode (being aggressive and bullying).
- Healthy adult mode: in which the client's mature executive functions dominate and they can gather information, make rational decisions, express compassion and take care of self and others.

Case study: schema coaching

Wilber was a lawyer with a major firm who had rapidly risen to the top remuneration band because of his hard work and astute legal opinions. He came to coaching looking downcast and tired. He explained that he felt bad because he had missed his daughter's fifth birthday party because he was working on an urgent matter. His normally accommodating wife was furious when he arrived home late on the Saturday evening and said that something had to change! He was referred to coaching by the head of People and Culture from his firm.

Wilber was the youngest of five sons who had grown up in a loving but very competitive family. All the brothers played cricket well and frequently practiced in the back yard. Wilber remembers his oldest brother practicing his spin bowling which involved him delivering the ball slowly but with a nasty change in direction after bouncing. There were several times when the young Wilber was hit with the ball and laughed at by his brothers.

He did well at school and at university and was an A grade student. He worked very hard and started doing 'all nighters' at university in preparation for exams. Wilber was a summer intern for a large law firm during his university days and loved the office companionship and competition.

The coach started using the GROW (Goal, Reality, Options and Way forward) model of coaching and Wilber was able to set some goals to limit his work hours and to spend a reasonable amount of time with his wife and children. This went well until he won a large and urgent piece of work from a merchant bank. The client was demanding and at times aggressive. Wilbur foolishly agreed to a series of milestones that were almost impossible. Then in the middle of the work, a senior staff member left the firm and Wilbur was in trouble! The next four coaching sessions were filled with cathartic downloading about the unreasonable demands that he faced. Wilbur also discussed his alcohol consumption and stated that he was drinking four or five glasses of wine every night. This worried both him and his wife.

The coach suggested that schema coaching would be of value at this point and discussed the framework for schema analysis and case conceptualisation. Wilbur readily agreed that this approach sounded useful.

After a two-hour session of intense working Wilbur and the coach had agreed on the following. Wilbur suffered from two maladaptive schema, unrelenting striving and needing approval. He had two adaptive or positive schema, success and stable attachment. His coping style was schema surrender as he had unthinkingly adopted a lifestyle of overwork and an excessive dependence on the client's approval. His schema modes were vulnerable child (feeling miserable about this life) and detached self-soother (the excessive use of alcohol).

The schema analysis proved to be an enlightenment for Wilbur who prior to this was completely unable to understand why an able and intelligent person like himself was so trapped and unhappy. The analysis proved to be a very useful basis for case conceptualisation and Wilbur worked for the next six months with the coach to address his challenges. After this time Wilbur decided to leave the major firm and start a firm of his own as a way of getting out of the competitive law firm culture. Over time the combination of schema coaching and change in lifestyle was very effective in enabling Wilbur to achieve a much better work life balance.

The schema octagon

To provide an overview of the schema approach the following graphic has been developed which sets out the nine key elements of schema coaching (adapted from McCormick 2023a).

The element at the centre of the octagon, limited reparenting, is a process that aims to help heal the unmet needs of the client and involves the coach giving a great deal of themselves to overcome the, often unintentional, inadequate childrearing received by the client. The elements in italic on the right, plus relapse prevention, are the basic techniques which can be used by experienced coaches without psychotherapy training and the elements on the left in bold are ones best undertaken by coaches with psychotherapy or specialist training. All these elements are explained in detail in the subsequent chapters of the book.

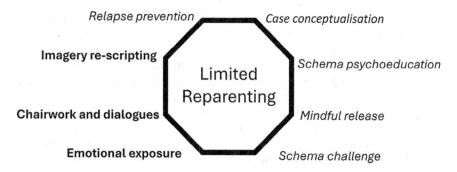

Figure 3.1 Schema octagon.

Reflective practice exercise

The following exercise aims to help the reader to think more deeply about the topic and to consider applying the approach in their own practice.

Thinking about yourself, which of the early maladaptive schema seem to apply to you?

Example: I can see the Unrelenting striving is very relevant to me.

Thinking about yourself, which of the positive schema seem to apply to you?

Example: I can see the Success and Developed Self are relevant to me.

Which of the three coping styles apply to you?

Example: I have surrendered to my schema.

Which of the schema modes do you get into?

Example: My critical parent drives me to work harder and achieve more. My vulnerable child feels miserable that I do not relax and enjoy life more.

What do you want to do now that you have undertaken your schema analysis?

Example: I want to read the rest of the book and see which techniques I can apply to myself. It is exciting to think about.

Key learning points

1   Coaching has developed through a series of waves that have reflected the advances in the psychology of learning. First-wave cognitive behavioural coaching was based on the theory of classical condition or pairing of stimulus with response from Pavlov and others. The second wave was based on operant conditioning and emphasised the importance of reinforcement shaping behaviour. Third-wave cognitive behavioural coaching was based on more complex approaches such as that seen in schema therapy.
2   Schema coaching, based on schema therapy, uses three levels of analysis to build a broad understanding of the client Firstly early maladaptive and positive adaptive schemas which involve enduring patterns of feelings, thoughts and behaviours that often have a lifelong impact. Coping mechanisms or methods that clients try in vain to use to control, eliminate or reduce the schema pain and frustration. Lastly schema modes or mood state changes which are moment by moment responses to everyday issues.

Discussion topics

What are the theoretical foundations of first-, second- and third-wave coaching?
What are the key differences between cognitive behavioural therapy and schema therapy?
What are the key differences between schema therapy and schema coaching?

Suggested reading

Jacob, G., Van Genderen, H. & Seebauer, L. (2015). *Breaking negative thinking patterns: A schema therapy self-help and support book.* John Wiley & Sons.

McCormick, I. (2023a). An introduction to schema coaching techniques, part 1: The schema octagon. *The Coaching Psychologist*, 19(1), 27.

Roediger, E., Stevens, B. A. & Brockman, R. (2018). *Contextual Schema Therapy: An integrative approach to personality disorders, emotional dysregulation, and interpersonal functioning.* New Harbinger Publications.

Young, J. E., Klosko, J. S. & Weishaar, M. E., (2003). *Schema therapy: a practitioner's guide.* Guilford Press.

Chapter 4

Case conceptualisation

This chapter outlines the collaborative process that coaches and clients use to better understand the client's challenges that have brought them into coaching. This process is called case conceptualisation and within the schema analysis framework it has three levels of evaluation: early maladaptive and adaptive schema, coping styles and finally modes. This analysis is used to provide a descriptive scaffold so that the coach and client can better understand the presenting issues and then design a coaching plan. A semi-structured interview guideline for schema case conceptualisation is set out in the chapter as well as a guideline for mode case conceptualisation. The chapter includes several case studies showing the value of different case conceptualisation approaches. It also includes a reflective practice exercise, key learning points, discussion topics and suggested further reading.

What case conceptualisation is

Case conceptualisation is the joint process used by the coach and client to draw up a mental map of the issues that the client has brought to coaching. The original case conceptualisation concept was developed within counselling but is now frequently employed in a wide range of therapies (Passmore & Oades, 2015). Case conceptualisation aims to both describe the client's issues using a model or theory of personal change and to make connections between these issues and the model. After the explanations about the causes and the maintenance of the presenting issues have been identified, they are then used to develop change options and processes (Kuyken et al., 2009).

In schema case conceptualisation, the schema analysis framework, consisting of early maladaptive and adaptive schema, coping styles and modes, is used to provide an agreed description of the presenting issues. The schema framework also provides a basis for the coach and client to work collaboratively together to better recognize the causes and maintaining conditions relevant to the client's issues. This understanding is then used to develop schema coaching options that can be used to help the client address their underlying unmet needs.

DOI: 10.4324/9781003501824-4

Case conceptualisation is a fascinating, intellectual and emotionally stimulating process for the coach as it aims to organise and make sense of large amounts of complex information given to the coach by the client. The coach needs to understand this information, to identify the underlying patterns and themes, to present these patterns back to the client in a straightforward way and get mutual agreement about them. These patterns will include background context, specific triggering events, the resulting adaptive and maladaptive responses, the way in which the client has coped with these and the resulting mood or mode fluctuations. The process will also identify the strengths and challenges of the client which will be used to develop a set of coaching goals. The key skills in case conceptualisation are agenda setting, rapport building, committed listening, paraphrasing, pattern identification, providing clear explanations, expressing positive intent, questioning, providing feedback, encouragement and support (Kuyken et al., 2009).

The following topics are useful in schema coaching case conceptualisation as adapted from McCormick (2003b):

1 The presenting issues and why the client has come to coaching
2 The life history of the client and the patterns that emerge
3 The origins of these patterns and how they developed
4 The core childhood memories or images associated with these patterns
5 The likely adaptive and maladaptive schema
6 The current day triggers of the schema and the impact of them
7 The overall coping strategy of the client to the schema
8 The present moment mode changes that are visible in the session
9 The overall impact of the schema, coping styles and modes on the client
10 The goals that the client wants to achieve through schema coaching.

Schema case conceptualisation guidelines

A semi-structured guideline for case conceptualisation is set out below. In any initial schema coaching session, the coach can make the following statements or ask any of the questions below that are relevant to the client's situation.

Step 1: Coach's introduction

- Ensure that the client is comfortable and feels safe. Agree upon confidentiality.
- Explain the purpose of this session – which is to develop a deep understanding of what the client is bringing to coaching, their background, the formative stages of their life, the patterns that emerge from this, the impact of these patterns and how coaching can assist the client.
- Ask the client what they want to get out of coaching or what life might look like in a year's time if coaching was highly successful.

Step 2: Coach's initial questions

- Can you please tell me about your background, your ancestors, where and who you were born to?
- Can you tell me about the backgrounds and personalities of your parents?
- Tell me about your family, brothers and sisters, their backgrounds and personalities?

Step 3: Early childhood

- What was your early childhood like? Tell me about growing up and your primary or elementary school days.
- Overall, how did your early childhood impact you?

Step 4: Middle childhood

- What were your school years like? Tell me about growing up and your secondary or high school days.
- Overall, how did this part of your childhood impact you?

Step 5: Later childhood, early adulthood

- What were your university years like?
- What were your greatest challenges at this time?
- Overall, how did this time impact you?

Step 6: Early career

- Tell me about your first job – what did you do?
- How did it work out?
- Overall, how did your early career impact you?

Step 7: Later career

- What other jobs did you have? How did they work out?
- Overall, how did your later career impact you?

Step 8: Core childhood memories

- If you had to pick one core childhood memory or image associated with the pattern in your life, what would it be?
- Can you tell me in detail what happened?

Step 9: Schema triggers

- When you think about the patterns or schema that impact you, what are the typical triggers or 'emotional buttons' for you?
- What is the chain of events when you do get triggered.

Step 10: Lessons

- Having reviewed your life so far, what themes or patterns do you see in it?
- What are the lessons about life you have learned so far?
- If these are lessons that life has taught you, what would you like to achieve from schema coaching?

If the client had already been provided with information about schema, coping styles and modes, the coach may ask the client to describe their life in these terms. Alternatively, the coach may suggest a pattern of schema, coping and modes, then ask the client if that sounds relevant to them.

Case study: a schema case conceptualisation

Muhammad was an IT project implementation manager with a hesitant disposition who was involved in the sale of his company's products. He came to coaching after having sold a major software package and its subsequent implementation to a medium sized accounting firm. Muhammad was very pleased with the sale until his manager contacted him and said that the client had rung and asked if the project team undertaking the implementation could be led by someone other than Muhammad. The client had explained that they felt Muhammad lacked the confidence to deal with the senior partners in the accounting firm. Muhammad was deeply frustrated by the news. His manager had said that he would go back to the client and explain that project managers of Muhammad's calibre were very scarce and that replacing him would be extremely difficult.

The next day his manager came back and said that the client had accepted that Muhammad would lead the implementation but that to address the confidence issue he would be offered executive coaching. Muhammad had mixed feelings, delighted that he would lead the job but suspicious about the coaching.

In the first session Muhammad quickly developed a sound relationship with the coach and so overcame his suspicion about executive coaching. The coach noted his quiet manner and often hesitant language and Muhammad agreed that he did come across like this but felt he was very capable of leading the implementation team. The coach then suggested two sessions of social skills training with a focus on direct eye contact, more direct expression and engaging voice modulation. Muhammad could see the value of these subtle style changes and said he would practice these whenever he could.

In the following session Muhammad came back disappointed because while he had tried to implement the style changes, he felt extremely uncomfortable and inauthentic doing so. He said that he felt that there was something deeper holding him back but that he was unsure of what this was. The coach then explained the schema approach and the idea of early maladaptive schema and Muhammad said he was very interested in trying this type of coaching.

While undertaking the case conceptualisation, it became clear that Muhammad's parents were very socially isolated as they had emigrated from India and had settled in a city without other family members or social support. They were both successful professionals but as an only child Muhammad had spent much of his childhood alone and feeling lonely. This resulted in him being very cautious in developing friends. After much discussion with the coach Muhammad felt that the abandonment schema was highly relevant to him and his challenges. As a result, the next series of coaching sessions focused on understanding and challenging the feelings, thoughts and behaviours that were generated by the schema.

The case conceptualisation resulted in a clear focus on the inhibiting factors that generated his hesitant social style. Only when considerable progress had been made in this area did Muhammad feel that he was ready to return to the social skills training, which when implemented was highly successful. The case conceptualisation had resulted in a clear direction for the coaching and had dispelled any suggestion that Muhammad was unwilling or unmotivated to undertake the behavioural changes.

At the three months follow up Muhammad was very pleased with his progress as the software implementation project was going very well and the client was pleased with the results. Muhammad felt that the coaching had uncovered a deep-seated issue and helped him gain self-confidence which he believed would be very valuable as his career progressed.

Coping styles

As seen in Chapter 3 schema coaching employs three levels of analysis to build a deep understanding of the client – these levels are: early maladaptive and adaptive or positive schemas, coping styles and finally modes which can be defined as follows:

1   Early maladaptive schemas are unhelpful enduring patterns of feelings, thoughts and behaviours. By contrast, adaptive or positive schema are long-standing patterns of successfully handling life's challenges.
2   Coping mechanisms are ways that clients use to try in vain to control eliminate or reduce the schema pain and frustration.
3   Schema modes or mood states are the moment-by-moment client responses to everyday issues.

So far in this chapter the case conceptualisation has focused on the schema level. However, it can also be useful for the coach to understand how the client is coping with the schema. Has the client simply given in to the schema and accepted it as part of themselves – the schema surrender coping style? Is the client trying to avoid any situations or circumstances that may trigger the schema for example taking a very undemanding job to avoid the chance of failure – the avoidant coping style? Alternatively, is the client using the schema compensation coping style so is attempting to do the exact opposite of what the schema would indicate. For example, a client suffering with the pessimism schema may regularly engage in high-risk sports to demonstrate their optimism to themselves and others.

McCormick (2022) noted that the most frequent coping style seen in schema coaching is surrender. However, it can be useful for the coach to consider if either of the other two coping styles are in play in order to develop a full picture of the client's challenges.

Mode mapping

Mode mapping is a collaborative formulation process in which the coach and client draw up a map of the client's mood states to understand their triggers, sequences and relationships.

In schema coaching, mode or mood shifts are less common than they are reported to be in schema therapy (McCormick, 2022). However, the mode concept is still a very useful part of case conceptualisation. Roediger et al. (2018) suggests six steps in the case conceptualisation of modes that have been adapted for schema coaching and set out below:

1   The coach introduces the idea of schema modes to the client, e.g., "We have seen how your challenge often leads you to fluctuate between frustration and powerlessness, would it be useful for you to understand more about this?".

2   The coach can then ask the client what they have learned so far about their mood or mode changes or can summarise the case conceptualisation, e.g., "You have told me you have a savage inner critic that seems to stop you from acting and makes you feel powerless – is that right?"

3   The coach then communicates that idea that these mode changes are critical to the development of the client's challenges, e.g., "These mode changes seem to be very important in messing things up for you – is that right?".

4   If the client and coach agree, the coach can go on to describe how the client may have coped with these difficult modes, e.g., "As your inner critic is so powerful, has it stopped you acting and achieving what you really want?".

5   The session can then move on to the coach teaching the client about the healthy adult mode, e.g., "I have found that many clients can reduce the

impact of the inner critic by strengthening what we call the healthy adult. Would that be useful for us to explore?".

6   Finally, the coach can ask permission from the client to start the experiential phase of schema coaching, 'Shall we start to work together to build your healthy adult?'.

When to use what type of case conceptualisation

Set out below are three types of case conceptualisation: schema-focused, coping styles and mode-focused case conceptualisation.

- Schema-focused case conceptualisation: this is most useful when the client's presenting issues are deep seated and long standing. These types of client challenges are often most clearly observed when the client has tried a range of coaching or therapeutic approaches and has still not been able to address the issues satisfactorily.
- Coping styles case conceptualisation: this is rarely needed in coaching as most clients have simply given in to their schema and so are using the surrender coping style. However, when the coach finds a highly complex client who is still clearly within the coaching population (that is someone having a reasonable degree of psychological, social and vocational stability) then a collaborative coping styles case conceptualisation can be useful. This type of conceptualisation is almost always used in conjunction with the schema-focused assessment as the coping style directly relates to how the client is dealing with the schema.
- Mode-focused case conceptualisation: this is most useful if the client's presenting challenges are rapid and difficult to control shifts between mood states e.g. moving from interest in a colleague's comments to anger and hostility towards them in a few seconds.

It is useful for coaches to be familiar will all three types of case conceptualisation but in my experience working with executive coaching is that schema-focused case conceptualisation is the most commonly used.

Case study: mode-focused case conceptualisation

Ophelia was the CEO of a physical fitness app start-up company. She had a background in IT and marketing which served her well in her leadership role. Ophelia came to coaching shortly after a successful major capital raise by her company. She was starting to undertake more detailed tactical planning to implement the overall business strategy that had been developed and agreed with her Board of Directors. The presenting issue she brought to coaching was her relationship with the Head of Digital for the company, Liam. Ophelia described him as brilliant, highly committed but deeply frustrating. She said that Liam was very insensitive to other people's needs but very sensitive to his own wants and needs. This made Liam a difficult leader for his digital team. He was inclined to be moody and would lash out for no apparent reason at others yet be 'mortally wounded' if others defended themselves and objected to his unkindness. Ophelia had tried a range of tactics to deal with the situation including running a workshop to draw up a team charter which not only set out the company vision, purpose and values but also clearly outlined what appropriate and inappropriate interpersonal team behaviour was. This approach had a significant impact in the short term but slowly Liam's behaviour reverted to his norm. Ophelia was concerned as she felt she was running out of options to deal with Liam's behaviour. She had talked to the Chair of the Board about the issue, but he simply said that Liam was central to the success of the company and that she needed to find a way to deal with him.

In the first coaching session it became clear that Ophelia had a long history of success at school, university and in her career. She said that she had experienced a 'golden run' so far in her life with few hurdles or challenges that she could not deal with. This made the situation with Liam especially frustrating as she felt stuck and unable to deal with it. After describing the detail of the situation, the coach asked if she felt in some way her frustration over Liam was making the situation worse. She looked shocked at the suggestion but after a few moments of silence said that this could be happening, but she had not thought about it in this way. The coach suggested that they work together to map out the situation and what possibly could be going on and Ophelia said that this sounded very helpful.

They identified one critical problematic situation which was Liam's behaviour in senior leadership meetings and so decided to examine this in depth. Ophelia said a recent situation arose in the meeting when the Head of Sales said that she felt the responsiveness of the app was a problem for many customers and a serious potential break on new sales. She had hardly finished speaking when Liam launched into a tirade about the fact that it was not the app that was slow but the myriad internet traffic complications between the app and customer. The Head of Sales said she disagreed and the situation deteriorated to the point where Ophelia decided to halt the meeting and rescheduled for the next day. Everyone in the senior team left the meeting with bad feelings, especially Ophelia.

The coach asked Ophelia to identify what she was feeling at the time when Liam started talking and then again when she rescheduled the meeting. She said that initially she had felt anger, even rage, but this had quickly turned to powerlessness and a strong need to escape at the point where she rescheduled the meeting. The coach started to map out the situation. On the left he drew a box that outlined the situation – senior management meeting when there is a criticism of the app's performance. Then he drew two circles the first labelled angry mode and the second escape mode and drew an arrow between them.

Ophelia said that she felt this captured the situation well and added in angry mode she would think to herself "Shut up Liam" and in escape mode would think "Get me out of here". The coach then drew a third circle labelled healthy adult and asked Ophelia what her healthy adult would do at the point where Liam started to get defensive. Ophelia thought for a few seconds and said, the healthy adult would notice the anger and in a calm and measured way interrupt Liam and suggest that this was not the right type of discussion for this meeting, according to the charter that the organisation had drawn up. If the Head of Sales had started to respond in a defensive way, she would also suggest that this was not appropriate for the meeting. She would then ask the Head of Sales to write a brief one-page report on the extent of the problem, the number and nature of the complaints that had been registered. She would then ask Liam to assign a capable staff member to do an objective analysis of the response time of the app under a range of different conditions. Ophelia's healthy adult could then say the team would discuss this once more when this additional information was available and move on to the next agenda item.

The coach asked Ophelia if she felt that understanding her healthy adult and strengthening this would stop her mode shift from anger to powerlessness. Ophelia said she certainly felt that would help.

The next three coaching sessions were spent working to strengthen Ophelia's healthy adult and to practice managing the angry and powerless mode states. Ophelia was a very capable CEO and was readily able to make the changes once she had a clear way to see the process in the mode map.

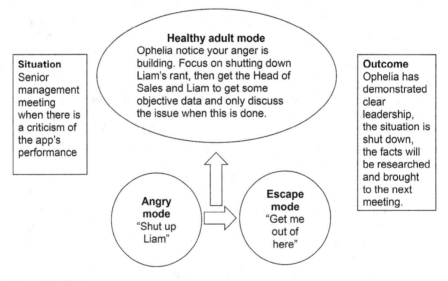

Figure 4.1 Mode map.

Mode case conceptualisation guidelines

A semi-structured guideline for mode case conceptualisation is set out below:

Step 1: Coach's initial questions and actions

- What is it that you would like to work on today?
- That situation appears to be one that has caused you to experience a range of emotions – is that right?
- Would you like to explore this situation in more depth?
- The coach then explains the nature of modes and mode mapping.

Step 2: Coach's subsequent questions and actions

- Tell me in detail what happened in the situation that bothered you.
- What were the emotions that you experienced and when? Try and use just one word to describe the emotion if you can e.g. sad, angry, frustrated, etc.

Step 3: Mode mapping

- Now that I understand the situation and the emotions, shall we try and map it out to see if we can understand it better?
- The coach and client work collaboratively to draw up the mode map.
- The coach asks, "Does that seem to capture the situation and what happened?".

Step 4: The healthy adult

- Now we understand how the situation evolved, how do you think your healthy adult would suggest that you react?
- Or, if the client is struggling to answer this question:
- What do you think a wise friend would advise you to do under this circumstance?
- Coach adds the healthy adult response to the mode map.
- Would you like to work on ways to strengthen your healthy adult further?
- The coach and client then work on ways to do this.

Step 5: Lessons and actions

1 Having reviewed the mode map what did you learn?
2 What actions do you want to undertake as a result of our mode map?
3 You have now outlined your action plan, shall we both write that down and follow up on it in our next session?
4 Is there anything else you want to cover today?

5   Overall, how useful was the mode map in helping you understand and alter what is going on?

Reflective practice exercise: Case conceptualisation

Consider the range of schema that is set out in Chapter 3. Which of these is most relevant for you?

> Example: I can see the relevance of the needing approval and self-sacrifice schema for me.

Work through the schema case conceptualisation guidelines set out above and build a deeper understanding of your schema.

> Example: I can see that my needing approval schema started very early in my childhood and is now triggered in conflict situations where I feel uncomfortable.

What actions do you want to take as a result of this analysis?

> Example: I will talk to my supervisor about this and see what she advises me to do.

Consider the range of modes that is set out in Chapter 3. Which of these is most relevant for you?

> Example: I can see the relevance of the vulnerable child mode for me.

Work through the mode mapping guidelines set out above and build a deeper understanding of your schema.

> Example: I can see that I want to build my healthy adult further so that I can better support my vulnerable child.

What actions do you want to take as a result of this analysis?

> Example: I will also talk to my supervisor about this and see what she advises me to do.

Key learning points

1   Case conceptualisation is the joint process used by the coach and client working together to draw up a mental map of the issues that the client brought to coaching.

2 Case conceptualisation is a fascinating, intellectual and emotionally stimulating process for the coach as it aims to organise and make sense of large amounts of complex information that have been given to the coach by the client.
3 Case conceptualisation can usefully be done at a schema, coping style or mode level of analysis.

Discussion topics

Review your current coaching case load and discuss which clients you think have a presenting issue where the schema case conceptualisation method could be useful? Why?

Reflect on your current clients and discuss which clients you think using mode mapping could be useful with? Why?

Suggested Reading

Green, T. C. & Balfour, A. (2020). Assessment and formulation in schema therapy. In *Creative Methods in Schema Therapy Advances and Innovation in Clinical Practice*, pp. 19–47.
McCormick, I. A. (2023b). Case Conceptualisation using Schema Coaching Analysis: An Illustrative Case Study. *Coaching Psychology International*, 16(9), 1–7.
McCormick, I. A. (2023c). Schema coaching techniques, part 2: Schema case conceptualisation and psychoeducation. *The Coaching Psychologist*, 19(2), 4–12.

Chapter 5

Foundation techniques

This chapter is designed to help coaches decide how to operate within the limit of their professional competence and which schema techniques they should train in, be supervised in and then use. It discusses the development of the coaching profession and the range of training undertaken by coaches. It outlines the similarities between coaching and clinical psychology (and psychotherapy) which include an emphasis on behaviour change and the importance of the relationship between the professional and client. The differences between the two professions include the fact that coaching focuses on work-related issues and skill building as compared with the clinical psychology primary focus on non-work issues. The chapter explains the range of schema techniques which are best suited to coaches who are not trained in clinical psychology, counselling or psychotherapy. A key purpose of the chapter is to help coaches decide which schema techniques they should use. It also includes an illustrative case study about a non-clinically trained coach using the schema approach, a reflective practice exercise, key learning points, discussion topics and suggested further reading.

The scope of practice of coaches

The major international professional coaching bodies codes of conduct and ethics make it clear that coaches need to remain within the scopes of practice which they have been trained and supervised to operate in. For example, EMCC Global states that:

> "Members will operate within the limit of their professional competence. Members should refer the client to a more experienced or suitably qualified practicing member where appropriate".
>
> (EMCC Global, 2024)

This chapter can help coaches decide how to remain within the limit of their professional competence and which schema techniques they should train in,

DOI: 10.4324/9781003501824-5

be supervised in and then use. The training of coaches is one critical determinant of professional competence.

Training for coaches

Coaching can be a highly lucrative profession with demands for this service rising rapidly over the last two decades. However, coaching is an unregulated profession with a broad range of individuals entering it with a wide array of experience and qualifications (Diller et al., 2020). This situation has led to a great range of different services being offered under the same banner and so there are challenges for the profession, including:

- The difficulty of separating coaching from other services such as mentoring
- The intangibility of what is offered
- The fact that these coaching services can differ widely depending on the coach's individual background (Greif, 2018)

A study that used 2,267 coaches and 754 personnel managers who engage coaches for their organisation, asked participants to answer a survey about coaching quality and quality control. The results indicated that more coach training led to both better self-perceived and other-perceived coaching quality. However, coaching experience did not relate to other-perceived coaching quality or quality control. So, the authors concluded that the level of training but not experience, is an important factor when selecting coaches (Diller et al., 2020).

Coach training helps coaches to learn both a range of relevant skills and self-reflection competencies (Diller et al., 2020). Carden et al. (2023) suggest that coach training is growing rapidly as a service despite few coaching training programmes being evidence-based. Diller et al. (2020) suggest that self-reflection, supervision and evaluation are ways to enhance the quality of coaching services.

Most coach training is based on competency models that have been constructed using expert opinion, but these are only about 50 per cent accurate in predicting client behaviour change (Boyatzis et al., 2023). These authors used a sample of 240 coach-client dyads with 60 different coaches to test which competencies predicted client behaviour change over two years. The effective coach competencies were achievement orientation, adaptability, emotional self-control, empathy, organisational assessment, and influence. While more research is needed to confirm this finding, the study does raise the important issue of how much current coach training, which is based on broad competency models, is superfluous and if more focused evidence-based training would be far more economical and effective.

The range of training for coaches

Coaching training is offered by a range of providers including the following:

- Post-graduate university programmes e.g. the Master of Science in Coaching for Behavioural Change from the Henley Business School (Henley, 2024)
- Certificate courses in coaching e.g. the Foundations of Coaching Certificate from Weatherhead School of Management (Weatherhead, 2024)
- Private approved coach training providers, e.g., those accredited by the International Coaching Group Inc (IGC, 2024)

Coaching versus clinical psychology and psychotherapy

There are several similarities between coaching and clinical psychology/psychotherapy that include an emphasis on behaviour change and the importance of the relationship between the professional and client. Differences include the coaching focus on work-related issues and skill building as compared with the clinical psychology/psychotherapy typical focus on non-work issues. Coaching focuses on the employee while clinical psychology focuses on the individual client. The client bases differ with the coaching population having higher levels of functioning compared with the clinical population. Clinical psychologists generally have more authority and power in the relationship while coaching is more of a collaboration of equals. Coaches are generally paid by the organisation and clinical psychologist by the client (Gebhardt, 2016)

Foundation techniques versus advanced techniques

Based on this explanation it can be concluded that coaches who also have clinical psychology or psychotherapy training are better placed to work with clients who have more complex challenges using advanced techniques. Coaches without these qualifications are more suited to using foundation techniques which are detailed in the next four chapters of the book. These are:

- Case conceptualisation
- Schema psychoeducation
- Mindful release
- Schema challenge

The more advanced techniques are set out in Chapters 11 to 13. All coaches need to understand the limits of their competence and refer on clients if they are not trained and capable of assisting them. This topic is covered in depth in Chapter 2. The advanced coaching techniques are:

- Emotional exposure
- Chairwork and dialogue techniques
- Imagery re-scripting
- Relapse prevention

Case study: a non-clinically trained coach using the schema approach

Daphne had undertaken her coaching training with an ICF accredited coach provider, and this had equipped her with a range of the skills designed to empower individuals to achieve their goals and find fulfilment at work and in life. The programme was a mix of online, live, and interactive sessions and Daphne found it very useful because it built both her confidence and competence. She came to develop a sound understanding of the ICF core competencies and ethics, along with a broad range of personal change coaching techniques. Daphne felt that she was developing the sort of capability and experience she needed to be an effective coach.

However, after a few months of coaching she started working with an executive who reported being overwhelmed with stress and stuck in a dead-end job. Daphne used her newly found skills to build a strong relationship with the client and to start to encourage him to see his situation as an opportunity rather than a problem. This went well for three sessions, then on the fourth the executive told her that he had had an argument with his manager and felt very bad about it. When Daphne enquired further, he said that he had driven home from work yesterday and that he had been tempted to cross the median line in the road and drive into the path of an oncoming truck.

When hearing this, Daphne shuddered and started to feel sick. She believed that she had a good relationship with the client but now felt unsure of what to say or do. After a few moments of disengagement, she recalled her training. She knew she needed to help her client to access a qualified clinical psychologist or psychotherapist. She listened attentively and allowed her client to vent for some time and then explained that she was a coach and not a psychologist. She made it clear that if his desire to harm himself was strong then he needed to see a clinical psychologist and not a coach. The client looked rather puzzled and asked what the difference was. Daphne was able to explain this and say that she had a very good relationship with a clinical psychologist who had a practice in the same building. She could strongly recommend this person and was happy to help him to get an appointment if this is what he wanted. He was silent for quite some time and then said, "I love my kids, so I better get some further help!". Daphne listened with a great sense of relief particularly because the client reassured her than he would be safe in the interim period. Those ethics classes that she had attended and found boring, had suddenly become important and real.

Self-reflective exercise on undertaking coaching

As a coach have you had formal training in coaching? Yes or No. If you answered No you should not be undertaking coaching until you have finished this training.

Have you undertaken coaching to deal with some of your own challenges? Yes or No. If you answer No you should undertake a period of personal coaching.

Do you belong to a professional coaching or other relevant organisation and adhere to their code of ethics? Yes or No. If you answer No you should not be undertaking coaching until you have a clear understanding of professional and ethical standards.

Do you screen for high-functioning clients? Yes or No. If you answer No you should undertake training so that you can identify clients who are not suitable for coaching, and you should refer these clients on.

Do you have a qualified clinical psychologist or other trained psychotherapy professional who you can refer on to if needed? Yes or No. If you answer No you should find a suitable person to refer on to.

Do you have regular ongoing supervision from a trained coach? Yes or No. If you answer No you should find a qualified supervisor.

Do you have regular reflective practice-based professional development? Yes or No. If you answer No you should not be undertaking coaching.

Key learning points

1   Coaching is a lucrative profession with increasing demands, but it is an unregulated profession with a wide range of individuals entering the profession with varying experiences and qualifications.
2   Coach training leads to better self-perceived and other-perceived coaching-quality. Self-reflection, supervision, and evaluation are ways to enhance the quality of coaching services.
3   Coach training is offered by postgraduate university programmes, certificate courses in coaching, and private coach training providers.
4   Coaching focuses on work-related issues and skill building, while clinical psychology typically focuses on non-work issues. The coaching population usually has higher levels of functioning compared with the clinical population, and coaches are generally paid by the organisation and not by the client.
5   Coaches with clinical psychology or psychotherapy training are better placed to work with clients who have greater and more complex challenges using advanced techniques. However, all coaches need to understand the limits of their competence and refer on to other professionals when appropriate.

Discussion topics

Consider the range of training that has been undertaken by members of your group. What do individuals feel was the best and worst parts of the training they undertook?

Discuss the differences in capability and competence of coaches who have training in clinical psychology, counselling or psychotherapy and those who do not have this type of training.

It has been argued (Boyatzis et al. (2023) that most coach training is based on coaching competency models that are only about 50 per cent accurate in predicting client behaviour change. Does this mean that most coach training is unnecessary?

Suggested Reading

Boyatzis, R., Liu, H., Smith, A., Zwygart, K., & Quinn, J. (2023). Competencies of coaches that predict client behavior change. *The Journal of Applied Behavioral Science*, 00218863231204050.

Carden, J., Jones, R. J. & Passmore, J. (2023). An exploration of the role of coach training in developing self-awareness: a mixed methods study. *Current Psychology*, 42(8), 6164–6178.

Diller, S. J., Passmore, J., Brown, H. J., Greif, S. & Jonas, E. (2020). Become the best coach you can be: The role of coach training and coaching experience in workplace coaching quality and quality control. *Organisationsberatung, Supervision, Coaching*, 27(3), 313–333.

Chapter 6

Schema psychoeducation

This chapter sets out the process and knowledge content that the coach uses to help the client understand the detail of any change process. In the schema coaching context psychoeducation provides the client with the knowledge they need to better understand their schema and to begin to deal with them. The type of psychoeducation used in schema coaching is closely related to that used in many other forms of therapy and counselling. Psychoeducation is used in many situations including in serious mental disorders, e.g., dementia, schizophrenia, clinical depression, anxiety disorders, eating disorders and personality disorders. This chapter includes an illustrative case study, a reflective practice exercise on the impact on individuals of gaining therapeutic knowledge, key learning points, discussion topics and suggested further reading.

Psychoeducation in coaching and therapy

Psychoeducation is a specific structured method that involves the coach or therapist sharing a range of relevant and important information with their client about the nature, challenges, causes and steps to resolution of the presenting problem (Powell et al., 2022).

Early psychotherapies placed little focus on client education because the therapist was considered to be the expert rather than the client. This approach has now changed and many therapists use psychoeducation because they understand the importance of the client's own expertise in understanding their own background and experience (Swift & Parkin, 2017).

Psychoeducation is used in many areas such as with serious mental disorders, including dementia, schizophrenia, clinical depression, anxiety disorders, eating disorders, and personality disorders (Tay et al., 2016).

In the schema coaching context psychoeducation provides the client with the knowledge they need to better understand their schema and to begin to deal with them. The type of psychoeducation used in schema coaching is closely related to that used in many other forms of therapy and counselling (McCormick, 2023c).

DOI: 10.4324/9781003501824-6

There is a lack of sound research into the effectiveness of psychoeducation in coaching, with many studies merely describing or supporting its use. An example of this is Reger et al. (2013) who advocated the use of psychoeducation provided through smartphones for improving homework compliance during prolonged exposure therapy.

McKay and Kemp (2018) recommended psychoeducation for coaching clients to enhance their understanding of habit formation, neuroplasticity and brain-based change. They suggested that demonstrating the power of habit formation and the simple reality of neuroplasticity could provide clients with the confidence they needed in their ability to be more cognitively flexible and to overcome beliefs about their brains being fixed or "hardwired".

Jarosz (2020) argued that psychoeducation had an important role in building emotional intelligence in coaching, but the author's work did not isolate the impact of the psychoeducation from the many other elements involved in the coaching.

Outside the coaching area there is some evidence of the utility of psychoeducation. Dahl et al. (2019) in a systematic review of the area found that psychoeducation led to reported improvements in symptoms and behaviour by parents of attention deficit hyperactivity disorder (ADHD) clients. This is important because ADHD is a common neurodevelopmental condition in adolescence and childhood, so psychoeducation could have a broad impact.

Pollio et al. (2006) used a one-day "family survival" psychoeducation programme to better inform the relatives of patients who had been diagnosed with a serious mental illness such as major depression, schizophrenia, or other affective disorders. Eighty-three families completed a self-report questionnaire and an open-ended "problem list" before and after the workshops. The study found positive changes and the authors concluded that the approach demonstrated promising achievement of the study outcomes.

Duman et al. (2010) undertook a study to measure the effectiveness of psychoeducation for in-patients with chronic mental illness. They used a questionnaire completed by 46 patients before and after the programme. The results demonstrated that patients could learn complex material in a short, well-structured training programme during their typical short in-patient stay.

A systematic review and meta-analysis of research into the impact of psychoeducation on developing social skills of young people with ADHD was undertaken by Powell et al. (2022). Their review examined ten studies with 943 participants and found that psychoeducation significantly improved social skills in young people. However, the effect sizes were small.

It has been suggested that psychoeducation is an important part of the treatment of clients diagnosed with schizophrenia (Herrera et al., 2023). Psychoeducation has also been found to increase treatment adherence, decrease relapse rates, and hospital readmission while increasing functioning, satisfaction with treatment and overall quality of life for patients with schizophrenia (Xia et al., 2011).

It appears that psychoeducation improved adherence to treatment protocols in pharmacotherapy because clients understood why the therapist had made their recommendations and how these would assist them. Clients were also able to ask questions and so reduce their concerns about the recommendations (Unterecker, 2019).

By contrast, Brouzos et al. (2021) reviewed eight studies with 719 subjects and found that psychoeducation for adults with post-traumatic stress disorder had neither statistically significant nor clinically important effects compared to treatment-as-usual in decreasing symptoms. However, they suggested that despite these findings its use should be further investigated.

In a conceptual analysis study that has direct relevance for psychoeducation and case conceptualisation, Słysz and Soroko (2021) asked how psychotherapists built client understanding and what conceptual tools (assumptions, ideas) they used. The authors produced fourteen conceptual maps from three male and 11 female psychotherapists and found four major themes in these maps: the importance of parental figures, the impact of basic assumptions about the "world order", the relevance of the patient's inner world and the need for the psychotherapist to maintain a tolerance of inconclusiveness. They suggested that dynamic, hypothetical and adjustable assessment for therapeutic purposes seems personally engaging and helpful to patients. The greater the level of understanding about the client's inner world the more both psychoeducation and case conceptualisation can be tailored to the clients' needs.

Psychoeducation in schema coaching

While there is a porosity of evaluative research on the impact of psychoeducation in schema coaching it has been argued that it may help clients to:

- Better appreciate the importance of basic human needs, how needs are met on not met, and therefore how long-term patterns of feeling, thinking and behaviour develop.
- More fully understand how their schema are central to their current challenges.
- Comprehend how their schema developed and impacted on their lives (Rafaeli et al., 2011).

A useful method of psychoeducation for schema coaching clients is to suggest that they read the book *Reinventing Your Life: The Breakthrough Program to End Negative Behavior… and Feel Great Again* (Young & Klosko, 1994). This book is an easily understood guide on how to overcome 11 common, self-defeating emotional schemas or what the authors call lifetraps. The book explains the most common childhood origins of schema, how these patterns impact self-defeating thinking and behaviour patterns as well as choices of life, such as the selection of a life partner. Each chapter covers one lifetrap in detail and contains a short questionnaire to assist the reader to see if this schema is relevant to them. The book also explains the typical childhood origin of each of the specific lifetraps, how these manifest themselves in life and in relationships, and it provides specific strategies for change. The book contains self-help exercises and a range of helpful illustrative case studies.

Clients can also be provided with useful information on schema coaching. Chapter 16 of this book contains a short guide designed to be handed out to clients.

Case study: psychoeducation

Zac was a change management consultant who came to executive coaching after finishing a one-year fixed term contract with a government department. The role had been extremely demanding and Zac had ended up working 60- to 70-hour weeks for months on end. At the end of the contract, he felt depleted and depressed. In his first coaching session he said he wanted to find better work-life balance but said that he was torn between his burning ambition to make a significant difference in the world and his need for rest and restoration. During this first session, he developed a strong effective collaborative relationship with the coach and was able to freely express his feelings.

In the second session Zac said that he was feeling worse than before he came to coaching and was starting to become extremely concerned about what he described as his chronic insomnia. He said he had been to see his doctor but was very disappointed not to get any medication to help him sleep but also at his doctor's comment that "Surely, you must be getting some sleep each night!".

At this point the coach asked if Zac had read much about sleep and if increasing his knowledge in this area would be useful. Zac felt it would help him. The coach explained that sleep issues were very common, with some estimates suggesting that one in three individuals suffers from insomnia at any point in time. Zac appeared relieved to know that he was not alone with this problem. The coach then went on to explain the four stages of sleep and the importance of rapid eye movement sleep. Zac was very curious. The coach then explained that for the average 20-year-old, the person would move in and out of the stages of sleep and could expect to wake up once or twice in a night. However, these periods of physiological wakefulness were typically very short and the person would not recognise that they had woken up at all. As the person got older the sleep patterns changed and by the time the individual was 70, they could expect to wake up five or six times a night, to know they were awake and for it to take some time to get back to sleep. This was just the reality of getting older. The coach also explained that these patterns may have had some evolutionary advantage because many thousands of years ago when tribes slept in communal areas it was highly beneficial if some members of the tribe were periodically awake and therefore alert to possible attacks from outsiders.

The coach also explained that most people were very poor at understanding whether they were actually awake or asleep in the depths of the night. The person's brain could be very active and when they woke, they felt certain that they had been awake for hours, yet physiologically they had been sound asleep. Zac said he found that extremely helpful and that he immediately felt a bit more relaxed about his insomnia.

The coach then went on to talk about the value of good sleep practices. She suggested that Zac read a book called *Insomnia: How to sleep better* (Lack et al., 2003). The key ideas of good sleep hygiene were avoiding caffeine, nicotine and alcohol, not eating too late, having a regular night-time ritual, not going to bed too early and not having a phone within easy reach of the bed. The coach and Zac developed an action plan based on the most relevant of these ideas and Zac left the session feeling much more optimistic.

Zac started the next session by saying that he was much less worried about his sleep patterns and although he felt better, he still did not sleep well. Interestingly he also felt that this reduced level of anxiety had helped him think through his career options in a much more rational way. He had decided that he would look for another change management contract but take a role that involved more data analysis and less direct client management. He felt that this type of work would keep him intellectually stimulated, earn him satisfactory money but also allow him to pursue a much more balanced lifestyle.

The coach felt that the psychoeducation about the nature of sleep had been the critical factor in assisting Zac to deal with a range of important career and lifestyle challenges.

Schema psychoeducation guidelines

It is recommended that the coach use the following guidelines to implement schema psychoeducation:

1   Carefully and collaboratively understand the client's challenges. Remember the presenting issue is not necessarily the most important one.
2   Check that the client wants to understand more about this issue.
3   Research the relevant psychological literature on this issue using Google Scholar or a similar internet-based tool.
4   Assess the evidence that your identified approach works or that the information that you are about to give the client is correct.
5   Identify a range of articles or books that are at the client's interest and reading level which can be recommended.
6   If necessary, produce a one-page graphic summary of the issues based on the research.
7   Present the material to the client and check the relevance and impact for them.

Reflective practice exercise: psychoeducation

Think about a book or other source of information that has had a significant impact on your life. Describe the key ideas.

Example: I recently read a book 'Let go now: embracing detachment' by Karen Casey and found it very helpful in assisting me to reduce my worry about things that I cannot control.

Why were these ideas so powerful for you?

Example: They were powerful because I was better able to set boundaries in my life and so be more relaxed and productive.

How much psychoeducation do you use in your coaching?

Example: Up until now I have been focused on helping the client find their own solutions but now, I see there is a balance to be achieved between guiding and giving.

What are some areas where you feel you want to learn more so that you can provide your client with better psychoeducation?

Example: Sleep is an area I want to learn much more about.

Key learning points

1 Psychoeducation is a structured method that therapists and coaches use to share information with clients about their challenges, causes, and steps to resolution of presenting problems.
2 Despite the lack of sound research on the effectiveness of psychoeducation, authors have suggested that it has utility in improving adherence to treatment protocols, increasing treatment adherence, reducing relapse rates, and hospital readmission, as well as increasing functioning, satisfaction with treatment, and overall quality of life.
3 Psychoeducation in schema coaching may help clients to better understand the origin, importance and impact of their schema and provide hope that they can improve their overall quality of life.

Discussion topics

Consider how much each of your group members uses psychoeducation in their coaching. Discuss how they wish to improve in this area.

Discuss how clearly the coaches in the group know and can explain the effectiveness of the coaching techniques they use.

Selected readings

Lack, L., Wright, H. & Bearpark, H. (2003). *Insomnia: How to sleep better.* ACP Publishing.

Young, J. E. & Klosko, J. S. (1994). *Reinventing your life: The breakthrough program to end negative behavior... and feel great again.* Penguin.

In this volume: Chapter 16: A Clients' Guide to Schema Coaching.

Chapter 7

Mindful release

Mindfulness involves seeing the current moment and building awareness of thoughts, feelings and bodily feelings without judgment. This chapter explains how mindfulness practice can be used to assist clients to better deal with their unmet needs and the challenges uncovered by schema coaching. It sets out the functional mechanisms behind the impact of mindfulness. It outlines a range of different mindfulness-based therapies and the effectiveness research on these. The chapter provides a warning that mindfulness is not for everyone and that some individuals may have adverse effects. There are detailed instructions on how to use mindful release in schema coaching, an illustrative case study on the value of mindfulness, a self-reflective exercise, key learning points, discussion topics and suggested further reading.

What mindfulness is

Mindfulness is an active state of mind that involves the individual observing the present moment, being aware of thoughts, feelings and bodily sensations without judgment, and noticing distractions without blaming themselves (Gardner et al., 2023).

Mindfulness is based on the philosophies of the Eastern contemplative traditions and is often seen as being at the centre of Buddhist meditation. Thera, (2005) has called mindfulness the "heart" of Buddhist meditation. Meditation can be seen as the exercise needed to build the skill of mindfulness (Kabat-Zinn, 2003). Mindfulness is, however, more than meditation as it involves deliberately focusing on the moment-to-moment experience throughout daily life. Mindfulness is 'paying attention in a particular way: on purpose, in the present moment, and non-judgmentally' (Kabat-Zinn, 1994). It is easy to understand mindfulness by contrasting it with mindlessness. The former is focused attention, and the latter occurs when attention and awareness are scattered and diffuse.

DOI: 10.4324/9781003501824-7

Mindfulness meditation has three attributes:

1   Intention, which is the expressed desire by the person to achieve something specific during meditation, this may include to find quietness, to experience peace, etc., and may change over time.
2   Attention, which means carefully focusing on the moment-by-moment, internal and external experience.
3   Attitude, which is the general qualities the person brings to the mindfulness which may include compassion, curiosity, critical enquiry or openheartedness (Shapiro et al., 2006).

Mindfulness-based therapies

There are four widely respected therapies that employ mindfulness-based approaches:

- Mindfulness-Based Stress Reduction, which is an eight-week training programme originally created for chronically ill patients. However, it has been applied to a range of dysfunctions and conditions such as anxiety, coronary heart disease, cancer pain and depression (Nehra et al., 2013).
- Dialectical Behaviour Therapy, which is a structured psychotherapy using mindfulness, acceptance and distress tolerance, emotional regulation, and interpersonal effectiveness to assist clients to improve the quality of their lives (Linehan, 1993).
- Acceptance and Commitment Therapy is an evidence-based intervention that uses mindfulness, acceptance and a range of psychological strategies to reduce the intensity of symptoms. It also uses values-based commitment to behaviour-change to increase psychological flexibility (Hayes et al., 1999).
- Mindfulness-Based Cognitive Therapy for depression, which consists of an eight- session programme that has been demonstrated to improve the recovery from depression and reduce relapse (Segal et al., 2002).

Mindfulness based interventions involve the cultivation of a present-moment focus over a sustained period and not just in a single mindfulness induction.

(Goldberg et al., 2022)

The benefits of mindfulness

In a comprehensive meta-analysis, Khoury et al. (2013) used 209 studies, with 12,145 participants, and found that at the end of treatment, mindfulness-based therapy was significantly more effective than psychological education, supportive therapy, relaxation procedures, and imagery or suppression techniques.

There were no significant differences between mindfulness-based therapy and traditional cognitive-behavioural therapy, other behavioural therapy or pharmacological treatments. Effect sizes for mindfulness-based therapy were larger when used with psychological disorders than for physical or medical conditions.

The authors concluded that mindfulness-based therapies were moderately to largely effective for a range of psychological problems, especially for reducing anxiety, depression and stress.

Mindfulness-based therapy has been applied in a wide range of areas. In a recent systematic review and meta-analysis, Mao et al. (2023) used 61 studies with 4,229 patients to assess the effectiveness of mindfulness-based interventions for ruminative thinking and found significant intervention effects. However, mindfulness-based interventions were not significantly better than cognitive behaviour therapy. The authors found that there were significant positive impacts for clinical patients, healthy adults and students who suffered from depression or cancer. The authors concluded that mindfulness-based therapy can improve ruminative thinking and enhance mindfulness. Treatment groups with a higher number of females showed greater improvement while there were no significant differences in the age of subjects or the duration of intervention.

A comparison was made of the effectiveness of unified protocol for transdiagnostic treatment and mindfulness-based schema therapy on posttraumatic avoidance and chronic illness-related cognitive fusion in patients with breast cancer using a semi-experimental study with pre and post-test design. Forty one patients were randomly divided into two experimental groups and a control group. Unified protocol for transdiagnostic treatment and mindfulness-based schema therapy were used in ten weekly sessions with the control group only having two educational sessions. There was a significant difference between the treatment and control groups but there were no differences in effectiveness between the unified protocol treatment and mindfulness-based schema therapy. The authors concluded that both treatments can be used to reduce cancer patient psychological problems (Ghayour Kazemi et al., 2023).

Goldberg et al. (2022), in a systematic review of 44 meta-analyses or random controlled trials of mindfulness-based interventions, found that these were more effective than control conditions for anxiety management, depression, weight/eating related conditions and psychiatric and psychological symptoms. These interventions improved the management of cancer, pain, physical symptoms, stress, sleep and well-being, but with small effect sizes. These interventions did not improve substance use and while they did improve self-report measures of health, they did not improve objective and physiological health measures. According to the review, the longer-term effects faded but were still positive for many conditions. The authors concluded that mindfulness-based interventions are as useful as other therapies for stress, depression, smoking, psychological symptoms, but not for a range of other dysfunctions (Gardner et al., 2023).

Impact

Mindfulness-based interventions may not be effective for everyone, regardless of age, gender, or culture. While many studies show benefits, they are not consistent across all groups and it is unclear what works best for each individual (Gardner et al., 2023). Mindfulness may be as effective as relaxation training or yoga for reducing distracting thoughts. Combining different mindfulness practices may be more helpful than using any one approach alone. The authors argue that the diversity of mindfulness-based interventions available can lead to confusion. Additionally, the quality of research methods and therefore evidence is a concern, with studies that show no or negative effects being less likely to be published. Many studies have small samples, no control groups, and rely on self-report data, which may not accurately measure the effects of mindfulness interventions (Gardner et al., 2023). Clearly more methodologically sound research is needed to understand the complexity of the issues.

Adverse effects

The adverse effects of mindfulness are not often reported in the literature. However, Farias et al. (2020), in a systematic review, suggested that meditation can be unhelpful or even harmful in some circumstances. Some individuals who do not have a history of mental health problems reported unhelpful reactions to meditation including anxiety, body pain, depression, fear, stress, re-experienced trauma, gastrointestinal and memory problems. It is not clear who is most at risk of adverse effects.

Britton, (2019) suggested that mindfulness can be too much of a good thing and is not universally helpful. Van Dam et al. (2018) suggest that care needs to be taken to not over-state the benefits and that some practitioners might use other evidence-based treatments or regular aerobic exercise. which has well-established benefits for physical and mental health.

A useful research-based list of meditation-related experiences that can be distressing or associated with impairment in functioning can be found at www.cheetahhouse.org/symptoms.

In conclusion mindfulness-based interventions can address various issues, but not all, and their benefits in some studies may be overstated. While not a substitute for other evidence-based approaches, mindfulness can be useful to improve the well-being of clients.

How mindfulness works

Research into the functional mechanisms behind mindfulness suggests that the following are relevant factors (Van Vreeswijk et al., 2014):

- Awareness: meditation can increase awareness in daily life and therefore lead to greater well-being.
- Decentering: this involves individuals coming to see thoughts as phenomena which are not necessarily true or important, they may not require action or any type of personal investment.
- Psychological flexibility: this involves being able to be more adaptable in the way in which individuals think about issues and in particular the way they process unpleasant and undesirable thoughts and feelings. It can involve clients allowing thoughts and feelings to exist without getting into counter-productive tactics.
- Values: clients can become more aware of what is most important in their lives and acting in accord with these.
- Emotional regulation: this involves clients allowing all emotions to be experienced and not automatically rejecting these or acting on impulse in accordance with these.
- Self-compassion: this builds understanding and sensitivity to oneself and contrasts sharply with the self-condemnation that clients often experience. It involves understanding that painful feelings are an inevitable part of human existence and so staying with these rather than running away from them can be very helpful.
- Brain change: extended periods of mindfulness meditation can lead to functional alterations in the brain that result in more adaptive cognitive and emotional processing.
- Attention and working memory: improving these abilities can lead to greater productivity and psychological functioning and a reduction in maladaptive thinking.

Mindfulness in schema therapy

In the book *Mindfulness and schema therapy,* Van Vreeswijk et al. (2014) present a comprehensive guide to using mindfulness to assist clients with deep seated maladaptive schema. The authors suggest that schema therapy has two phases: the initial assessment phase where the therapist and client collaboratively identify the schemas and modes, secondly, the transformation phase where a range of different interventions are used to address these schemas. This second phase typically draws on gestalt, psychodynamic, cognitive behavioural, and behaviour therapy to deal with past difficulties and traumas. Van Vreeswijk et al. (2014) suggest that mindfulness can be used as a new third stage to help clients let go of schema pain and impact. This involves the use of non-judgemental mindful attention focused on the client's schema to reduce the impact of inner conflict, unhelpful feelings and thoughts.

In the original group training format developed by the authors eight group sessions of 90 minutes plus two follow-up sessions were held. The groups included eight to 12 men and women aged between 18 and 65 years. The groups placed considerable emphasis on skills acquisition. Rather than having general discussions about personality problems the groups focused on just three members and their most influential schema and modes to work on during the whole course of the training. Focusing on these specifics allowed awareness and understanding to effectively be built. The first two sessions involved an explanation and practice of basic mindfulness techniques. In the third session clients practiced mindfulness awareness and letting go of painful memories. In the fourth session clients learned how to observe their schema and modes in action thus building awareness of these at a practical level. The fifth and sixth sessions involved participants learning to challenge their schema at a cognitive level and undertaking mindfulness-based mode work. Sessions seven and eight included exercises that helped to build the healthy adult and happy child modes. The final two follow-up sessions involved opportunities for participants to refresh their knowledge and undertake additional mindfulness exercises for their schema and modes.

Mindfulness in schema coaching

By contrast to the approach above, mindful release in schema coaching does not necessarily follow a set group format but does involve the use of the same techniques, often presented in the same order, but typically with individual clients. Coaches need to learn all the mindful release techniques and be ready to apply them, with the client's permission, at the appropriate time in coaching.

Indications and contra indications

When using mindfulness release techniques in coaching it is important to understand the relevant factors that will impact the success, or not, of the approach. The following positive indicators for the use of mindfulness techniques in schema coaching (adapted from Van Vreeswijk et al., 2014) include a willingness to:

- Deal with long-standing troublesome challenges
- Address problematic difficult to change ruminations and negative thoughts
- Address painful and troublesome emotions
- Improve the ability to deal with impulsiveness
- Address difficult social interaction patterns
- Undertake intensive schema coaching

By contrast the contra indications include:

- Disorders that mean the client is unable to concentrate on the mindfulness techniques

- Persistent learning difficulties
- An inability to invest the time needed for the mindfulness-based schema coaching
- Difficulties with finances, health, transport or other basics which mean the client is unable to attend the sessions

Mindful release guidelines

Below is a guide and not a set of rigid prescribed steps for the coach in using mindfulness technique to deal with early maladaptive schema. Schema coaching is usually undertaken in a one-on-one format with some clients coming to coaching having already learned meditation, some progressing rapidly and others more slowly. So, unlike the group format above, the sequence and timing of the steps below needs to be tailored to the individual client.

Step 1: Case conceptualisation

1   The coach should start by building a powerful and collaborative relationship with the client. This provides the foundation for all further work.
2   Part of the relationship can be the case conceptualisation (see Chapter 4). This involves understanding the client's background, their challenges and the causes of these.
3   When relevant, the schema coaching approach involves the coach working collaboratively with the client to identify the likely early maladaptive schema that are impacting the client's well-being. In addition, the coach may help the client to identify their schema coping styles and modes (see Chapter 3).

Step 2: Psychoeducation

1   The coach then introduces the concepts of mindfulness-based schema coaching and checks that the client sees these as relevant and important.
2   The coach needs to make use of the indications and contra-indications of the mindfulness approach as set out above.
3   Care needs to be taken to ensure that if the client has any adverse effects during the mindfulness coaching, that they feel comfortable in immediately letting the coach know this so the process can be halted and modified.
4   The key concepts at this stage are:
    a   The purpose of coaching is not a way to remove or get rid of emotions but is a means to help the client have a different and more productive relationship with these.

b   Providing the background to early maladaptive schema, coping styles and modes and the collaborative identification of these, where relevant.

c   An introduction to mindfulness as a process of paying attention to the present moment in a non-judgmental way.

d   Discussing the value of mindfulness as a process to help with decentering – that is beginning to see thoughts as phenomena which are not necessarily true or important; building psychological flexibility or the ability to be adaptable in the way the client thinks and processes unpleasant and undesirable thoughts and feelings; emotional regulation, that is allowing all emotions to be experienced and not automatically rejecting these or acting on impulse in accordance with these; self-compassion which involves building understanding and sensitivity to oneself and contrasts sharply with the self-condemnation that clients often experience; building greater attention and working memory which leads to greater productivity and psychological functioning and a reduction in maladaptive thinking.

Step 3: Mindfulness training

1   This can start with a simple mindfulness of the breath meditation which involves focusing on the air flowing in and out of the lungs and returning to this when distracting thoughts arise.

2   The client may need reassurance that everyone has intrusive thoughts during meditation, and this is not only normal but actually helpful as it gives the individual the opportunity to watch the thoughts and let them go.

3   The client is asked to watch the arc of thoughts as they arise and fall away.

4   The homework from the session is to practice the meditation.

5   The coach should suggest that even five minutes a day is a great start to getting into the rhythm of meditation. A modest initial target is important as this helps to build a sense of achievement for the client.

6   The homework from the session is to practice the meditation.

Step 4: Body scan meditation

1   The session should start with a review of homework and the fulsome praise of whatever time that the client has spent in meditation.

2   The coach may need to further reassure the client that thoughts during meditation are perfectly normal and actually useful.

3   The client is then introduced to the idea that just as they can let go 'top of mind' thoughts during meditation, they can use the same process to let go of unpleasant sensations and memories such as those that arise as a result of the person's schema.

4   The client is then taught a simple body scan meditation which involves focusing on different parts of the body and mindfully noticing the sensations.
5   The important issue at this point is to help the client build greater bodily awareness so that later when they need to identify and let go of painful memories, they have a clear idea of where in their body the tension builds. This helps a great deal in assisting them to simply watch the tension and let it pass.
6   The homework from the session is to practice the meditation and build greater bodily awareness.

Step 5: Everyday mindful awareness and release

1   The session should start with a review of homework and praise for whatever time has been spent in meditation.
2   This session should include mindfulness breathing, an exercise to use present moment awareness to start to reduce the impact of painful memories.
3   The client is asked to remember a schema relevant scene and then identify where in the body they feel the resulting pain, then to watch it and see it slowly dissolve away.
4   It is important for the coach to start with a scene that is of low to mid-intensity. If the client starts with a very painful scene, they may become re-traumatised, and this would greatly harm their progress.
5   When the client has been through the cycle of body scan, imagining a scene, noticing the body sensations, and letting the painful emotions go, the coach should check that the emotional demand is only moderate and that the client is happy to repeat the process as homework.
6   If there is time the client can be introduced to other forms of meditation such as mindfulness walking.
7   The homework from the session is to practice only low to mid-level mindful release.

Step 6: Everyday mindful awareness and acceptance of self

1   The session starts with a review of homework and praise for whatever has been achieved.
2   The session then moves on to the five senses mindful awareness exercise – observing five things the person can see, four they can feel, three they can hear, two they can smell and one they can taste.
3   The coach then explains the importance of the mindfulness acceptance of self. This is the idea that effective long-term change can best be started by the client accepting themselves and letting go any critical or punitive thoughts that may arise about their schema.

4   The client is encouraged to go through the cycle of body scan, imagining a schema scene, noticing negative self-talk, accepting this, noticing any painful body sensations and accepting these. Again, the coach should check that the emotional demand is only moderate and that the client is happy to repeat the process as homework.

5   The homework from the session is to practice mindful release.

Step 7: Building the healthy adult and happy child

1   The session should start with a review of homework and praise for whatever has been achieved.

2   The coach then explains that building the healthy adult is a critical part of the personal growth process.

3   The client is asked to imagine that part of themselves that is mature, rational and balanced. Sometimes giving this healthy adult a name can be very helpful in strengthening it for example, Wise Bill or Belinda.

4   The client is then asked to do the body scan or other meditation, to imagine a moderately difficult situation that they face and then to imagine the healthy adult in the scene, thinking and acting in a mature and effective way.

5   If there is time, the client can be taught about the importance of the inner happy child and how this part of themselves can enhance their well-being and sense of enjoyment in life. Again, giving the happy child a name can be very helpful in strengthening it.

6   The homework from the session is to practice building the healthy adult and happy child.

Step 8: Focusing on the future and the maintenance of progress

1   The session should start with a review of homework and praise for whatever has been achieved.

2   The client is asked to identify any upcoming situations that might trigger schema pain.

3   These situations are discussed in detail and plans made to anticipate possible difficulties and to map out strategies for dealing effectively with these.

4   Strategies for maintenance of progress are then discussed and often the identification of supportive friends and family who can assist the client in the long term is very helpful.

5   The coach then asks the client if there is anything further they can help with and if the answer is no, the session can be ended.

6   If the client is unsure or concerned about the future a follow up session can be scheduled.

Case study: the value of mindfulness

Peter was a social worker employed by a housing charity and came to coaching to deal with a vague but persistent sense of failure. He had gained a Masters in Social Work and had been employed with the housing charity for seven years. He felt that his job was making a worthwhile contribution to society but somehow did still not enjoy the role. He had struggled to maintain romantic relationships in the past and had often felt lonely. After three sessions of solution-focused coaching Peter and the coach agreed that he was making little progress and so they agreed to start schema coaching.

The case conceptualisation revealed that Peter had a very dominant father who had belittled him as a child and had once said that he would 'amount to nothing'. Peter felt that this incident was at the heart of his failure schema. Peter's aim in coaching was 'to get his long dead father out of his head'.

When discussing ways to achieve this, the coach suggested mindful release and Peter thought that this sounded useful. Initially Peter struggled with meditation of the breath and said that he just could not stop the thoughts racing around inside his head. It took several sessions before the coach could convince Peter that thoughts during meditation were the norm. Peter was determined to deal with his sense of failure so persisted with the meditation.

When asked for a moderate level schema-relevant scene that Peter could use in mindful release, he chose to work on the circumstances around the breakup of his last girlfriend. This involved Peter repeatedly working late and forgetting to meet his girlfriend for a drink in the evening. She was furious with him and told him that he was 'a waste of space'. Peter had felt mortified. Despite the pain, sadness and sense of failure he experienced when imagining the scene, he diligently worked on identifying the body sensations associated with it and letting these go. It took about a month of persistent mindful release before Peter could feel that he was able to think about the situation without feeling like he was being 'kicked in the head'. The coach knew that he was making progress when he came to a session saying that breaking up with his last girlfriend was a 'lucky escape' and that her angry outbursts were toxic.

The coach then asked if Peter felt ready to move onto dealing with his relationship with his father. Peter took a deep breath and said, 'let's do it!' The scene Peter chose was the one where his father had said that he would 'amount to nothing'. Peter felt a tightness in his gut and a burning in his head when he pictured his father saying this. By this stage Peter had become skilled in staying with the painful feelings, rather than dismissing them, and watching them rise, peak and fall away. With the strong support of his coach, Peter persisted with the release of the painful memories and made slow but sound progress.

After five months of schema coaching Peter felt that he was starting to enjoy his work more and was even considering applying for a manager role in the organisation. He felt that the mindful release process had been very beneficial and that he had made real progress in getting his long dead father 'out of his head'.

Reflective practice exercise: Mindful release

Think about and write down a low to midlevel painful memory that you would like to work on.

> Example: I recall getting very drunk as a student and I remember being sick on my boyfriend's bathroom floor. I feel horrible about this incident even ten years later.

Learn a form of meditation from a reputable source.

> Example: I have chosen to use Mark William's Mindfulness of body and breath – he is an Emeritus Professor of Clinical Psychology at the University of Oxford and co-developed Mindfulness-based Cognitive Therapy. https://insighttimer.com/markwilliams/guided-meditations/mindfulness-of-body-and-breath-3.

Practice the meditation three or four times a week for a month and focus on watching your thoughts and bodily sensations rise up and fade away.

> Example: I have been practicing, but I am not sure how good I am at this. However, I do feel that I have made some progress. I can see that thoughts and feelings are sometimes important and useful and at other times they are just noise.

Practice using the meditation for five minutes and then remember a moderately painful schema relevant scene, identify where in your body that you feel the resulting pain, then watch the sensation and slowly see it dissolve away.

> Example: Initially I found this quite challenging and could feel that I did not want to remember the scene.

Continue to practice the mindful release until you feel that you can imagine the scene without undue stress. The aim is to enable you to get to the point where you feel you can easily tolerate the uncomfortable feelings.

> Example: Well, this has taken quite a lot of practice, more than I thought I would have to do – but I do feel a great deal better now and can certainly tolerate the uncomfortable feelings.

If at any time during this exercise you feel deeply uncomfortable, please find a professional coach or psychologist to work with.

Key learning points

1   Mindfulness involves observing the present moment, being aware of thoughts, feelings and bodily sensations without judgment, and noticing distractions without being self-critical.
2   Mindfulness is defined as paying attention in a particular way, on purpose, in the present moment, and non-judgmentally.
3   There are four widely respected therapies that employ mindfulness-based approaches: Mindfulness-Based Stress Reduction, Dialectical Behaviour Therapy, Acceptance and Commitment Therapy, and Mindfulness-Based Cognitive Therapy for depression. These all involve the cultivation of a present-moment focus through sustained meditation practice.
4   A number of comprehensive reviews have found that mindfulness-based therapy was significantly more effective than psychological education, supportive therapy, relaxation procedures, and imagery or suppression techniques.
5   Mindfulness-based therapy has been applied in a wide range of areas, including ruminative thinking.
6   However, mindfulness-based interventions may not be effective for everyone, and care needs to be taken when using these.
7   Mindful release in schema coaching does not necessarily follow a set group format but does involve the use of the same techniques as in mindfulness-based schema therapy, often presented in the same order, but typically with individual clients.

Discussion topics

Consider the types of people who you think might have an adverse effect to mindfulness and why this may occur.
Discuss a range of your current coaching clients and who you think mindful release may be useful for.

Selected readings

Bricker, D., & Labin, M. (2012). Teaching mindfulness meditation within a schema therapy framework. In *The Wiley-Blackwell Handbook of Schema Therapy: Theory, Research, and Practice*, pp. 259–270.

Segal, Z., Williams, M., & Teasdale, J. (2018). *Mindfulness-based cognitive therapy for depression.* Guilford Press.

Van Vreeswijk, M., Broersen, J. & Schurink, G. (2014). *Mindfulness and schema therapy: A practical guide.* John Wiley & Sons.

Chapter 8

Schema challenge

This chapter sets out how coaches can help their clients to challenge the thinking processes that reinforce their unproductive schema. This process uses schema challenge cards which are based on the cognitive behavioural therapy approach which combines the fundamentals of both behavioural and cognitive psychology. Schema challenge aims to reduce the severity of distress for individuals who suffer from a range of dysfunctions including depression and anxiety. The chapter provides detailed instructions on the use of the challenge process. A small sample of effectiveness research on cognitive behavioural approaches is set out. The chapter includes an illustrative case study on using schema challenge to deepen the readers understanding of the technique, a self-reflective exercise, discussion topics and additional suggested reading.

Schema challenge cards

Schema therapy was developed by Jeffery E. Young and colleagues in the early 2000s (Young et al., 2003) and some 20 years later McCormick (2022) developed schema coaching by utilising the schema therapy approach and adapting it for leaders, executives and others in the workplace. Schema coaching combines and integrates approaches from cognitive behavioural therapy, psychodynamic therapy, behavioural therapy, gestalt therapy and attachment theory.

Schema challenge cards are based on the principles involved in cognitive behavioural therapy, which combines the fundamentals from both behavioural and cognitive psychology. Cognitive behavioural therapy is an active form of intervention in which the therapist's role is to work closely with the client to find and implement effective strategies to reduce the dysfunctional thinking and so to help them to achieve their identified goals. This form of therapy is based on the fundamental idea that many common dysfunctions are caused by distorted thinking and maladaptive behaviours. Using this approach the therapist or coach helps the client to understand the unhelpful nature of their thinking and actions, to challenge their thinking patterns and to implement new effective thinking and behaviours (Beck, 2011; Palmer & Szymanska, 2018).

DOI: 10.4324/9781003501824-8

Schema therapy and coaching have both adapted the techniques of cognitive behavioural therapy so that these are focused directly on challenging maladaptive schema thinking. In schema coaching the cognitive behavioural approach takes the form of written schema challenge cards. These assist the coach and client to work systematically through a structured process of challenging the schema reinforcing thinking and to undertake helpful functional actions. The coach and client collaborate to develop a rational case against the schema. The client comes to understand that they are not flawed, inept or a failure but rather they have learned a set of ineffective ways to think and behave. It is not their fault and change can certainly happen.

The schema challenge process involves the following steps (adapted from Young et al., 2003):

1 The client talks over a challenging situation in which they understand their own thinking is hindering them.
2 The client identifies the painful emotion that arises in this situation. The coach encourages the client to use a single word to describe the emotion e.g. anger, disgust, sadness, surprise or fear.
3 The coach and client then work together to identify the situation that triggers this emotion. This step is important because it helps the client to see that emotions arise out of a specific context and do not 'just happen'.
4 The schema that caused the painful emotion is then identified. It can be useful for the client to give the schema a name – e.g., the black cloud or #fail. This naming helps the client to externalise and start to gain some distance from the schema.
5 Time is then spent working out how the schema leads to the distortion e. g. 'The moment I get into one of these situations the #fail starts to glow in big red letters, and I just give up'.
6 This is the step where the client explicitly challenges their schema thinking. They are encouraged to write out the detail of the challenge because typically they know that despite feeling bad, the reality of the situation is different from their current perception of it. For example, 'I feel like I am about to fail again, I feel terrible, but I do know that I can do this conference presentation'.
7 The client now writes out the evidence which supports this realistic view – 'I have given these presentations before, and I can do it again'.
8 The action that the client is going to take to defy their schema is then written down – 'I am going to get up on the stage and in a loud confident voice start my presentation'.

Having used schema challenge cards with clients for many years I find them very useful in allowing the client to shift their thinking patterns. However, some clients find the process difficult when it is undertaken for the first time so gentle empathic guidance is needed. I have found that most clients need to repeatedly use the cards before they can start to effectively confront their own thinking patterns in real time outside the coach's office. Overall, the process is very powerful as it helps the client to examine, externalise, and confront their largely unconscious and automatic thinking patterns. This collaboration with the coach provides a great opportunity for the client to critically examine their patterns of thinking and to act within a safe, empathetic and supportive coaching environment.

In their excellent book *Contextual schema therapy: An integrative approach to personality disorders, emotional dysregulation, and interpersonal functioning*, Roediger et al. (2018) sets out a slightly different schema challenge model based on the letters ABCDE. It is summarised below.

A is for the Actual scene: what is happening, what is the unwanted emotion and the trigger?

B is the Backstage scene: how has the schema caused or intensified the unwanted emotion?

C is the Change perspective: what is the nature of the unhelpful thinking generated by the schema and how can this be altered?

D is the Doing: what is the action plan that will enable the client to move from the current unproductive way to a more satisfying and productive approach?

E is for Effective: after the client has implemented the action plan what was the impact and was it effective?

Some coaches may find this ABCDE approach easy to explain to their clients and therefore easy for them to implement.

Challenging the range of schema

To provide some more detail on the nature of the schema challenge process – each of the commonly observed schema set out in Chapter 3 are presented below along with some useful challenges to them.

Unrelenting striving

Clients with this schema are typically extremely hard working and frequently believe that they must continue at this gruelling pace to meet their own and the organisation's very high-performance standards. They very often have a savage inner critic that drives them on to achieve more with its cruel and continuous condemnation.

The challenge to this unrelenting striving schema can include the idea that the client has already achieved a great deal in their life (this is almost always the case with senior executives) and that working harder may well damage their health and so reduce their capacity for further achievement. Clients may find comfort in knowing that their inner critic will never be satisfied no matter what they achieve, and that further striving may only make the critic more aggressive. The clients can challenge the idea that continuing at their usual gruelling pace is the only way forward and that having periods of total rest and restoration can be very helpful in achieving long term productivity.

Sense of failure

Clients with this schema believe that despite their achievements in life, they have failed, will fail, or that they are not as good or worthy as their peers. They often have a very persistent inner critic that is telling them that any success is just luck or a one-off or temporary.

The challenge to the failure schema is to encourage clients to look objectively at their lives and their accomplishments. Clients in executive coaching have typically achieved a great deal – for example they are often partners in professional service firms or senior leaders in corporates. These clients can also learn to challenge their inner critic which often has a limited number of 'tricks' which are applied endlessly. For example, the inner critic will say 'This is just a lucky break'. 'So you have done well so far but it will not last' or 'This success is happened by chance, and very soon someone will find you out and publicly shame you as a fraud'. Countering these internal arguments and building the healthy adult is critical for these clients. When clients do this, they often start to realistically acknowledge their achievements, praise their successes and soothe their insecurities.

Needing approval

This schema is commonly seen in executives with a sense of inadequacy or personal shortcoming and who despite their achievements, have a strong belief that they need too much attention approval or recognition from their manager, peers or team members. Executives who struggle to delegate, overly protect their team members from pressure and readily accept responsibility for problems outside their control, often suffer from this schema.

A useful challenge for these clients is to encourage them to ask their team members if they can handle more work. This directly confronts their reluctance to delegate and to protect and please their team. Seeing their team members tussle with difficult work problems can be painful for these individuals. However, seeing that despite these problems, the team can pull through, is very useful for them. When building the healthy adult, these clients can start to reassure themselves rather than search for external approval. They often need to learn to view and tolerate manageable amounts of stress and pressure in others without the need to protect them and so earn their approval.

Self-sacrifice

This schema is frequently seen in the health and other caring professions where they are constantly exposed to others with urgent needs. These professionals often feel that their own needs are unimportant and can be delayed because of the intense and critical needs of others. They often rationalise that they are self-sufficient but later can resent the demands of their job and their clientele.

Useful challenges include helping the client to see that they will not be able to serve their clients in the long term, unless they look after themselves. The airplane safety message 'Put on your own oxygen mask first, before assisting others' can be very useful. The healthy adult can help these clients to be more objective about their own limits and to balance demands with recuperation. They can learn to reassure themselves about the value of other team members helping and so feel less compelled to constantly sacrifice themselves and endlessly give more.

Lack of support

In this schema the client often has the belief that despite what they have done in life their significant others have not supported them enough, financially, emotionally or career wise. These individuals often work in organisations that are by their very nature insecure for example research groups that are totally dependent on external grants or commercial entities with only one customer.

In these cases, the client can be encouraged to look more objectively at who has already supported them in their careers. Almost everyone in any organisation who gets promoted or remains in a role in the long term does so through the support of their leaders and their team alike. The healthy adult can help these clients to have a more balanced view of these issues and to spend some time thanking those individuals who have already supported them, rather than ruminating on the lack of support. These clients are often deeply insecure and their healthy adult needs considerable encouragement to help them recognise their own achievements and successes. Most importantly, these clients can start to learn to accept themselves unconditionally without the need for constant support from others.

Excessive involvement with others

This schema means that the individual has little room to develop their own sense of self and is unsure of their own wants, desires, needs and value. In the workplace these clients can become very dependent on their manager or a peer for support and need their constant input or acknowledgement. They may feel unclear about their capabilities and their career direction.

Countering this schema can be done by encouraging the client to start to develop their own sense of self. Simple things like reading a range of books or eating at different cafes can help the person to decide what they like and dislike so building up a stronger sense of self. The healthy adult can help the person to emotionally separate themselves from the powerful other who has so often dominated their lives. They can start to either counter the internal voices that swamp them or find ways to slowly separate themselves from the important others if they are still around.

Pessimism

This schema is seen with clients who feel that they dwell too much on the betrayal, disappointments, losses, conflicts and failures of the past. They tend to minimise or trivialise the positive aspects of life.

These individuals typically have a strong inner critic who is constantly reminding them of life's losses, conflicts and failures. Helping the client to get a more balanced view of the good and bad in life is very important. Suggesting to the client that they limit their daily intake of bad news from all forms of media can be particularly important. Encouraging them to undertake random acts of kindness for others can also be useful in countering a pessimistic world view. Using the healthy adult to challenge the pessimism is critical and ensuring that the person can find sound evidence of the good in life is vital. The healthy adult can help the client to see that even in the worst of situations there is typically someone acting with courage and kindness.

Lack of spontaneity

Clients with this schema feel that they must control, contain and suppress their natural spontaneous actions, communications or feelings because others may not approve or because they may not be able to control their emotional expression once it starts. This is often seen in team members who work in a benign culture but who feel unable to express their frustration, disappointment, enthusiasm or vulnerability.

In this case building up the happy child mode can be particularly important. The client can be encouraged to find safe new ways to try out new spontaneous things. Going to different types of movies or watching a range of comedies on television can be a useful start. The healthy adult can help them to counter the need for control and emotional suppression. The client can be reassured that happiness in life often comes from small spontaneous actions such as talking to strangers, smelling the flowers or going on unplanned walks or holidays. It is also important that the client understands that spontaneous actions only come after practice – explaining this paradox can be useful to reassure them that their first awkward and self-conscious steps are the path to freedom of action and spontaneity. The healthy adult can provide assurance to the person that once unprompted actions start, they will be able to control their expression.

Feeling controlled

Despite having achieved a lot in their life and career people with this schema still often give up control of important areas in their lives to others. Individuals often give up this control because they believe that the dominant figure in their lives is 'always right' or 'must be obeyed'. This means that their own needs do not get met. However, often they try to avoid the criticism or disapproval of the other person. These individuals feel that their views are not important even when they are worthwhile.

These clients can be encouraged to start to take control in tiny areas of their lives, for example to wear clothes that may be just slightly more casual than expected at work, or quietly do things that not explicitly approved of by the dominant figure in their lives. Care needs to be taken that any such action does not backfire and cause anger or disapproval from the dominant other. Frequently, the individuals will have greatly exaggerated the level of obedience expected and so can learn to be rather more unconstrained without disapproval. The healthy adult can help these clients to decide on the important areas of their lives that they do want control over and the small steps they can take to achieve this.

The effectiveness of cognitive behavioural approaches

A small sample of effectiveness reviews of cognitive behavioural approaches is set out below.

In a comprehensive survey of 106 meta-analytic evaluation studies of cognitive behavioural therapy for 17 different disorders from aggression and anger to substance abuse disorder in groups including children and elderly adults, Hofmann et al. (2012) concluded that there is very strong support for the effectiveness of cognitive behavioural therapy for the treatment of a wide range of disorders. They found eleven studies that compared cognitive behavioural therapy to other treatments or to control conditions. Cognitive behavioural therapy was generally more effective than control conditions and had better response rates than the comparable treatments with only one study reporting lower response rates than comparison treatments. The authors concluded that cognitive behavioural therapy had very strong evidence of effectiveness in the 17 different disorders they studied from aggression and anger to substance abuse disorder.

In a systematic review and network meta-analysis Simon et al. (2023) compared the efficacy of a range of cognitive behavioural therapy treatment formats for insomnia using 52 random controlled trials. The authors found that for all delivery formats cognitive behavioural therapy was more effective than control conditions for insomnia severity, except when the therapy was delivered via smartphone. There were large mean differences between therapy and control conditions for individual onsite, group therapy, telehealth and guided bibliotherapy formats. The authors suggested that when other treatment formats are not available then the lower cost guided bibliotherapy could be very useful.

Cuijpers et al. (2023) used a comprehensive meta-analysis involving 409 trials with 52,702 patients to assess the effectiveness of cognitive behavioural therapy as compared with a range of control conditions, other psychotherapy types, pharmacotherapy and combined pharmacotherapy and psychotherapy for depression. They reported that cognitive behavioural therapy had moderate to large effect sizes compared with a range of control conditions, such as care as usual and waitlist. Although cognitive behavioural therapy was no more effective than pharmacotherapies in the short term, it was significantly more effective at the 6–12-month follow-up. They found no decrease in the effect size over time when comparing outcome studies between 2001 and 2011. Cognitive behavioural therapy was consistently more effective than other psychotherapies, but only by a small margin. This therapy was as effective when used as an unguided self-help intervention, in institutional settings, and with children and adolescents. The authors concluded that cognitive behavioural therapy appeared to be highly effective.

However, Johnsen and Friborg (2015) raised a note of caution by suggesting that their meta-analysis indicated that the positive impact of the effects of cognitive behavioural therapy on depression may be declining over time. They also found that where therapists used a manual to guide treatment there was a steeper decline in effect sizes than those that did not use a manual. The authors were unsure why the effects were declining. Clearly more research is needed to address these issues.

Case study: schema challenge

Alice had recently been made partner in a downtown medium sized law firm. She had grown up in a very wealthy family with two very successful parents and two older sisters who had each done extremely well. As the youngest child, she was highly social but rebellious. At school she did well but was often reprimanded for being naughty. At high school she immediately fell out with her form teacher who called her 'spoiled'.

At 16 she lost her mother who died in a tragic car accident and somehow Alice never seemed to recover from this. Her older sisters appeared to bounce back over time, but Alice never did. By 18 she was a regular drinker, and her alcohol consumption was starting to worry her father. This got so bad that she left home aged 19 after a terrible fight with her oldest sister.

Fortunately, she remained on good terms with her father who was supportive and financed her through law school. After leaving home she settled into an apartment with some mature law students and her study and lifestyle stabilised slowly.

She was recruited as a summer clerk into a large law firm during her university holidays and loved the work. She finally felt a sense of success and stability in her life. After five years she was put on a two-year fast track to partnership and although she was delighted by the opportunity and the status, she developed a sense of doom and impending failure that was hard to shake off. This was despite being, generally successful, very outgoing and establishing excellent client relationships.

A year after being a partner her sense of impending failure became overwhelming, so she found an executive coach to work with. In the first session she made it clear that she had a long-standing problem and wanted something much more than mere goal setting and support from her coach. She was very interested in schema coaching when this approach was suggested.

In the case conceptualisation phase, Alice and the coach agreed that she suffered from the failure schema and the coach suggested that they use schema challenge cards to begin to counter her thoughts of impending ruin. A summary of the use of schema challenge cards is set out below.

1   Alice chose to work on a paradoxical situation in which the trigger for feeling bad was entering a full partners meeting and being greeted warmly by several of the female partners. She said that this was such a strong trigger because she knew that everyone and particularly these female partners had very high expectations of her. Alice immediately felt that there was no way in which she could live up to these expectations.

2   The emotion she experienced was disappointment at herself for feeling such a failure.

3   She called her schema the Fearsome Failure Feeling.

4   Alice found it very easy to see how the schema caused her to exaggerate the impact of the situation. She knew that there were high expectations on all partners but that letting this feeling frighten her only made the situation worse. What was very important for her was to build her relationship with a core group of partners from other divisions so that she could get referrals and work with them in more complex matters that required a range of expertise.

5   Alice knew that despite her frightening feelings she needed to walk boldly into the partners' meeting and sit down next to someone who was both friendly and important to her.

6   After a lot of discussion Alice came to see that she would never have been invited into the partnership if she was a failure. She did have real strengths, particularly her ability to develop strong client relationships and win work. The facts did not support her sense of being a failure.

7   To reinforce her determination to overcome this challenge Alice agreed and then implemented a powerful action plan. Despite the discomfort and sense of vulnerability, Alice became friendly with a younger female partner and carefully, slowly disclosed to her the worry about not being

good enough and the feelings of being uncomfortable walking into partners' meetings. To her immense relief the other woman said she had felt exactly the same way when she joined the partnership and it had taken her two years before she really felt comfortable.

Alice was in executive coaching for about two years and worked on a wide range of issues including the death of her mother, her falling out with her sister, her past drinking patterns and so on.

At a two-month follow up session, Alice said that she was enjoying her work and life. She felt that the structured and logical schema challenge process had been an important part of the change.

Schema challenge guidelines

Below is a guide that is designed to help any trained and supervised coach to undertake the cognitive behavioural challenge of schema.

Step 1: Case conceptualisation

1   The coach should start by building a powerful and collaborative relationship with the client. This provides the foundation for all further work.
2   The coach should work together with the client to identify the likely early maladaptive schema and their impact on the client's thinking and behaviour. At this point identifying any positive schema can also be very useful.

Step 2: Schema challenge card completion

1   The coach can now introduce the idea of the impact of persistent and unhelpful thinking patterns on well-being and how a maladaptive schema can reinforce these patterns. In addition, the coach can help the client to see the value of their positive schema.
2   The coach needs to confirm that the client would find working in this cognitive challenge area helpful and then proceed on through the schema challenge card steps.
3   The questions to work collaboratively on are:

   a   What is an important and challenging situation that you want to explore where you believe that your thinking is not helping you?
   b   Use a single word to describe the primary emotion that you feel at this time.
   c   What are the critical elements in the situation that trigger this emotion?

d   What schema do you think is making this situation worse? Naming the schema at this point can be helpful to begin the process of externalising it for the client.

e   When and how did you learn the schema?

f   How does the schema distort your thinking and make the situation worse?

g   Despite feeling this way what is the reality of this situation – what is your healthy view?

h   What evidence do you have to support this healthy view?

  i   So, despite feeling this way what are you going to do differently?

i   What is your homework from this session?

Step 3: Further card completion

1   The coach needs to explore how the client found completing the homework challenge card.

2   The coach must complement them on any progress.

3   It may take several attempts before the client is ready to fully complete a card on their own.

Step 4: Application

1   When the client is confident at completing the cards, they can start to apply this same logical process in everyday situations.

2   It is best to start with situations that are easy for the client to complete and gradually work towards more challenging situations.

3   Praise from the coach for progress is important.

Step 5: Focusing on the future and the maintenance of progress

1   The session should start with a review of homework and praise for whatever has been achieved.

2   The client is then asked to identify any upcoming situations that might trigger schema pain.

3   These situations are discussed in detail and plans made to anticipate possible difficulties and to map out strategies for dealing effectively with these.

Key learning points

1   Schema coaching uses a variety of therapeutic approaches including cognitive behavioural therapy. This approach has been adapted within

schema coaching into schema challenge cards which the client uses to understand and counter their unhelpful thinking and behaviour.

2   The process includes the following:

a   The coach and client work together to identify the situation that triggered the painful emotion.

b   The client identifies the painful emotion that they want help on.

c   The key schema is identified and named.

d   Time is then spent working out how the schema leads to the thinking distortion.

e   The client learns to challenge the schema thinking and develop a healthy view.

f   The evidence to support this healthy view is written down.

g   An action plan to develop and maintain the new thinking is documented.

3   There is considerable sound evidence to support the use of this cognitive behavioural approach to help clients overcome challenges.

4   Clients may find that this approach needs much practice before they can complete a challenge card without the support of the coach and before they apply it directly in their lives.

Reflective practice exercise: Schema challenge

Read over the steps below and apply these to your situation.

1   Identify a situation that triggers a painful emotion for you.
2   Describe your painful emotion using a single word.
3   What is the key schema that impacts this situation?
4   How does the schema lead to the thinking distortion?
5   How can you challenge the schema thinking and develop a healthy view?
6   What evidence do you have to support your healthy view?
7   Now what is your action plan?

Example:

1   The situation: I was in an appointment with my doctor last week and trying to explain a medical issue. I became dumfounded and failed to explain my condition. It was deeply frustrating.
2   Self-hatred was the emotion.
3   Despite a good career and a happy family life I have always been haunted by a defuse fear of failure.
4   I can see that this fear makes me forget things and get confused. This is compounded by my inner critic who goes mental when I cannot remember things.

5   I need to accept that everyone forgets things from time to time. If I did this I would be more relaxed and be more coherent.
6   I see people forgetting names quite often at work. Hating myself for forgetting something is not helpful.
7   Before I go to my doctor next time, I will write a few notes on my phone and set out what I want to talk about. I will also do some yoga and start to mentally rehearse being calm and clear with my doctor.

If you have difficulties completing the card, who will you ask support from?

Example: I will talk this over with my coaching supervisor.

Do you wish to use this approach in your coaching? Where can you get extra training and support? How will you evaluate your effectiveness?

Example: Yes, I would like to use this approach. I will find a training course in cognitive behavioural therapy to go on. I will assess my effectiveness by how I feel using this approach and the feedback from my clients.

Discussion topics

Discuss a range of your current coaching clients and who you think schema challenge may be useful for.
Discuss what you think will be the easiest but also the most difficult elements of the schema challenge process to apply in your coaching.

Selected readings

Greenberger, D. & Padesky, C. A. (2015). *Mind over mood: Change how you feel by changing the way you think*. Guilford Press.
Neenan, M. (2018). *Cognitive behavioural coaching: Distinctive features*. Routledge.
Riggenbach, J. (2012). *The CBT toolbox: A workbook for clients and clinicians*. PESI Publishing & Media.

Chapter 9

Relapse prevention

All clients are susceptible to relapse at the end of schema or any other types of coaching. They can find their old challenges return when the pressure of life is intense. The aim of relapse prevention is to educate and prepare the client so they can reduce the recurrence of challenges after the end of schema or other coaching. Relapse prevention was originally developed for use with substance abuse clients, but it has relevance to all those who undergo change. This chapter sets out how to work with clients to identify the times of high risk and how to mitigate these risks. It includes an illustrative case study on how relapse prevention works. It also includes a reflective practice exercise, key learning points, discussion topics and suggested further reading.

Relapse prevention

Relapse prevention aims to educate and prepare the client so they can reduce the recurrence of unwanted challenges after the end of schema or other coaching. Relapse prevention was originally developed for use in therapy with substance abuse clients, but it has relevance to all those who undergo change. It has four main ideas. First, relapse occurs gradually with clear stages, so the goal is to help the client to recognise the earliest stage, when the prevention is easiest. Second, each stage of recovery has risks of relapse. Third, the key techniques of relapse prevention include risk assessment, withdrawal from risk, cognitive therapy and behavioural therapy such as relaxation. Fourth, psychoeducation is important and involves five rules: lifestyle changes are key as they reduce temptation, honesty is critical, help must be asked for at the right time, self-care and compassion are needed and don't bend the rules (Melemis, 2015).

Relapse prevention techniques

The relapse prevention techniques that are most relevant to coaching include the following which have been adapted from Marlatt and Witkiewitz (2005).

DOI: 10.4324/9781003501824-9

1   Risk assessment: to undertake this evaluation the client and coach spend time looking at the range and nature of upcoming events that the client will be likely to face. The events with the largest risk of relapse are identified and plans are set in place to mitigate the risk. For example, a client with the failure schema may not want to present their research findings to the senior management team because of a fear of possible criticism or harsh comments. Rather than spending time planning on ways of getting out of the presentation, the client and coach work on ways to reduce the opportunity for avoidance. These may include the client writing to their manager and making a clear commitment to do the presentation. The coach may even suggest that the client uses their smartphone to write and send the email during the coaching session!

2   Withdrawal from risk: once the client has identified the greatest risks, they work to find ways to withdraw from these situations. In this technique the art is avoiding the risk not avoiding the opportunity to face the schema. For example, the coach and client may find ways to quietly avoid an aggressive colleague who reinforces the client's feeling of failure but also to help the client to engage in planned manageable situations where they undertake challenges that involve some minor risks of failure. There is no benefit in the client being exposed to adverse situations when these will only make the schema worse.

3   Cognitive techniques: these involve ways to help the client to change how they think about situations and their schema. Challenging unhelpful thinking and strengthening the healthy adult is a critically important example of this that is relevant for almost all schema coaching clients. In doing this the client can start to set realistic and achievable goals, build motivation and so avoid relapse.

4   Behavioural techniques: these include using helpful alternative behaviours that can be undertaken when the risk of relapse is high. For example, when tempted to return to substance abuse the client might engage in strenuous exercise, group meditation, listen to loud music or phone an empathetic friend. Having a range of alternative healthy behaviours to undertake is a critical part of relapse prevention.

The effectiveness of relapse prevention

Relapse prevention is a frequently used cognitive-behavioural intervention for substance use. However, Irvin et al. (1999) reported that at that time the effectiveness research in the area was inconsistent and there was little agreement about the approach that led to maximum impact. In this early review the authors examined 26 published and unpublished studies with 70 hypothesis tests and 9,504 subjects. This early review suggested that relapse prevention was generally effective, especially for alcohol abuse and that it worked best when combined with medication.

In a meta-analysis on the effects of relapse prevention with offenders Dowden et al. (2003) reviewed 40 relapse prevention treatment studies and found moderate mean reductions in recidivism. The authors indicated that treatment programmes that set out the relapse prevention approach in explicit and clearly detailed ways were more effective than those that were vague or not as clear.

In a comparison of relapse prevention cognitive behavioural therapy versus medication for depression Rodolico et al. (2022) used five published trials and stated that medication and relapse prevention were both equally effective and that relapse prevention produced more positive results than when medication was started but then discontinued.

In a meta-analysis of relapse prevention strategies for depression and anxiety in adolescents and young adults Robberegt et al. (2023) reviewed research into these strategies for youth (13–25 years) who had suffered from depression or anxiety. They found 10 randomised controlled trials that examined depression and analysed nine of these. They were unable to find any relevant trials for anxiety. Over six to 75 months, relapse was 50 per cent less likely following psychological treatment compared with control conditions. Relapse over six to 12 months was less likely for youth getting antidepressants compared with those getting a placebo. The authors concluded that these prevention strategies reduced the risk of relapse for youth with depression, although further high-quality randomised controlled trials were needed.

Eadie et al. (2023) reported on a proposal to undertake a randomised controlled trial to assess the impact of developing and implementing a web-based relapse prevention psychotherapy programme for alcohol use disorder patients. They will use 60 adult participants who will be randomly assigned to receive ten sessions of web-based relapse prevention psychotherapy or face-to-face relapse prevention. The web-based approach will consist of ten modules and homework with personalised therapist feedback. Face-to-face relapse prevention will be ten one-hour sessions with a therapist. They report that this study will be the first to examine the effectiveness of web-based versus face-to-face relapse prevention. The outcome of this proposed research is not yet available.

Sharma et al. (2023) assessed the impact of the 'Quest' smartphone app for relapse prevention with alcohol dependent patients. They had 30 adults use the app for three months after their initial withdrawal treatment. The impact of the app was assessed using the mHealth App Usability Questionnaire. App use was compared with treatment as usual. The authors reported that for those that used the app both acceptability (65 per cent) and usability (5.8 out of 7) were high. Both treatment and control groups demonstrated a significant reduction in drinking at 30, 60 and 90 days compared with their baseline drinking. There was no significant difference between the groups who used or did not use the Quest App in the number of lapses and the days of heavy drinking. Clearly further research is needed into the utility of App use in relapse prevention.

Sala et al. (2023) undertook a meta-analysis on the predictors of relapse in patients with eating disorders. They reviewed 35 papers and found that higher care levels, psychiatric comorbidity, and higher severity of eating disorder psychopathology led to higher rates of relapse. Higher leptin, higher meal energy, higher change motivation, higher body mass index, a better response to treatment, anorexia nervosa-restricted eating rather than the binge purge type and older age onset led to lower relapse rates.

Killeen et al. (2023) studied the effectiveness of mindfulness-based relapse prevention in an aftercare programme for veterans with substance use disorder. They employed a randomised controlled trial to compare mindfulness-based relapse prevention to a 12-step facilitation aftercare programme following intensive treatment. Subjects in both aftercare groups maintained their alcohol and illicit substance use reductions during the aftercare. A total of 19 veterans returned to alcohol use during the treatment period and there was no difference between mindfulness and 12-step prevention groups.

In a large network meta-analysis of family interventions for relapse prevention for schizophrenia Rodolico et al. (2022) identified 28,395 studies and compared 11 family intervention models in 90 randomised controlled trials with 10,340 participants. They found that all family interventions, except crisis-oriented ones and psychoeducation with two sessions or fewer, decreased relapse significantly when compared with treatment as usual. The authors concluded that almost all family intervention models were effective in preventing relapse in schizophrenia.

In conclusion there is some evidence to suggest that for some populations relapse prevention techniques can be effective. However, the results are mixed. No relapsed prevention studies in coaching could be identified at the time of writing. There is a need for more well conducted research in the area.

Case study: relapse prevention

Ralph was an architect working on a large industrial complex. He had greatly enjoyed both his time at university and then working for a very large architectural firm. He had recently been made a studio principal and been put in charge of this large, complex and time constrained industrial project. However, over the last year he had suffered from increasing levels of distress with poor sleep, unhealthy eating patterns and excess alcohol consumption. The major cause of his stress was his relationship with the construction project manager for the site. The coaching started with a case conceptualisation and revealed a mild unrelenting striving schema. The coach taught Ralph deep muscle relaxation, which helped with his sleep and assisted him reduce his alcohol consumption to more healthy levels. At this point Ralph felt he had learned a lot and that he did not need much more coaching. The coach was concerned that relapse was very possible and asked Ralph if he was interested in one more session to undertake relapse prevention. Ralph thought this was a good idea.

The coach then undertook the four relapse prevention steps:

- Risk assessment: Ralph and the coach undertook a review of the range of upcoming events that were in Ralph's calendar. From this they decided that there were two high-risk events that were worth careful consideration. The first was a weekly progress meeting run by the construction project manager. After some discussion Ralph decided that he would do deep muscle relaxation in the morning before the meeting and at the end of this relaxation he would imagine himself dealing with the meeting in a calm adult manner. The second issue was dealing with a staff member who was not performing up to expectations. Ralph felt that he had been avoiding doing anything about this and made a firm resolution to firstly talk to his team's People and Culture Partner and understand the process that he must follow. Then within three working days he would have a frank discussion with the individual. Ralph later reported by email to the coach that he felt much better having undertaken the risk assessment and having a concrete plan.
- Withdrawal from risk: Ralph felt that a big risk for him was going to the drive-in liquor store on his way home from work. If he could avoid this temptation, he would do much better. The coach and Ralph then looked at the possible routes from the large industrial complex he worked on to his home. They agreed on a route that kept Ralph well away from the drive in and so avoided the risk.
- Cognitive techniques: the coach introduced the idea of the healthy adult and asked Ralph to adopt this mode and think about what else he could do to avoid drinking too much. Ralph came up with the idea that he needed to find something enjoyable to do that was not alcohol related. He felt that if he set himself a regular schedule of going to the movies once a week it would be a start to finding enjoyable non-alcohol related activities. The coach asked Ralph what else he could do and after some time Ralph said he had lost contact with a range of his friends and wanted to track them down and set up a much more regular set of coffee meetings or walks together.
- Behavioural techniques: Ralph thought this was important and decided that if he found himself craving for a drink he would immediately put on his headphones, listen to loud reggae music and go for a strenuous walk.

At the end of the session Ralph said it had been extremely helpful and that he felt that he now had a whole range of important practical ways to deal with his stress and manage his alcohol intake. He said the most important thing was that these techniques would greatly reduce the chance of any future relapse.

Reflective practice exercise: Relapse prevention

Identify a challenge that you have which seems to reoccur over time and that you want to work on. Write about it below:

Example: I enjoy drinking wine with meals on the weekend but am too often tempted to share a bottle of wine with my husband on Sunday nights and this is not good for my early Monday morning start.

Identify the high-risk situations where this troublesome challenge is likely to occur again in future. Pick out the situations with the largest risk of relapse and identify a plan to mitigate the risk.

Example: The high-risk situation is buying wine on Friday after work. If I buy two bottles there will be nothing left to drink on Sunday evening.

Is there some way you can avoid the tempting situation? Can you use this withdrawal from risk to help yourself?

Example: For the next month I will ask my husband to buy the wine and to only buy two bottles. If I am not in the liquor store, I will not have the temptation.

Spend some time getting in touch with your healthy adult, think about what else he or she could do to reduce any relapse.

Example: I have quite a well-developed healthy adult and I will openly talk to my husband about this issue and suggest that he purchases our weekend wine.

Can you use behavioural techniques to assist yourself? These include identifying helpful alternative behaviours that can be undertaken when the risk of relapse is high?

Example: Avoidance of temptation and getting in a new routine of not drinking wine on Sunday evening is so important.

What is your overall action plan?

Example: Have a discussion with my husband after work this evening and set in place the new agreement for the upcoming weekend.

Who can you use to support you in this plan?

Example: I am sure that my husband will support me on this one.

Key learning points

- Relapse prevention is an important aspect of coaching, aiming to educate and prepare clients to reduce the recurrence of challenges after the end of coaching.
- It is based on four main ideas: relapse occurs gradually with clear stages, each stage of recovery has risks of relapse, the relapse prevention techniques include risk assessment, withdrawal from risk, cognitive therapy and behavioural therapy.
- Relapse prevention involves five rules: lifestyle changes are key, as they reduce temptation, honesty is critical, help must be asked for at the right time, self-care and compassion are needed and don't bend the rules.
- Risk assessment helps clients identify the events with the largest risk of relapse and then helps them to set out plans to mitigate these risks.
- Withdrawal from risk involves the client avoiding high temptation situations.
- Cognitive techniques help clients change their thinking about risky situations.
- Behavioural techniques involve planning alternative things to do to avoid relapse.

Discussion topics

Review your current clients and identify the ones who you think are at highest risk of relapse after coaching has finished. What is it about these clients that makes them high-risk?

Is relapse prevention a relevant approach that you want to adopt? How will you learn more about this and who can supervise your work in this area.

Selected readings

Gorski, T. T. (1995). *Relapse prevention therapy workbook: Managing core personality and lifestyle issues.* Herald House/Independence Press.

Hedges, B. A. (2012). *Relapse prevention workbook.* https://archive.org/details/relapse-prevention-workbook.

Melemis, S. M. (2015). Focus: addiction: relapse prevention and the five rules of recovery. *The Yale Journal of Biology and Medicine*, 88(3), 325.

Chapter 10

Advanced schema techniques

This chapter introduces the most highly developed and complex schema coaching techniques and provides guidance on who should use these. It builds on Chapter 5 which assists coaches choose how to work within the bounds of their professional competence. The chapter explains the nature of clinical psychology, counselling and psychotherapy training and recommends that coaches with this type of training are more suited to using these advanced techniques. If a coach is not trained in clinical or counselling psychology or psychotherapy, it does not mean that the advanced techniques in this book are off limits. However, these coaches need to be careful and consider if and how they proceed in the area. Recommendations are made on how non-clinically trained coaches should proceed. The chapter contains a case study that illustrates the process undertaken by the author in his clinical and coaching training. The chapter also includes a reflective practice exercise, key learning points, discussion topics and suggested further reading.

The scope of practice of coaches

As stated in Chapter 5, the major international professional coaching bodies codes of conduct and ethics make it clear that coaches should only operate within the limit of their professional competence (for example, the EMCC Global code of ethics, EMCC Global, 2024). This chapter is designed to help coaches to decide how to operate within this limit and which schema techniques they should train in, be supervised in and then use. Having explained the foundation techniques earlier in the book, this chapter starts to explore the more advanced techniques and who should use these while remaining within the limit of their professional competence.

Complex schema techniques

Overall, this book aims to introduce coaches to a wide range of schema coaching techniques, with the first half of the book outlining procedures that any trained, supervised and ethically sound coach may be able to undertake.

DOI: 10.4324/9781003501824-10

The techniques discussed from this point forward in the book are more complex and therefore primarily recommended for those coaches who have completed clinical psychology, counselling or psychotherapy qualifications. The reasons for this recommendation are that clinical and related qualifications provide: extended tertiary education and training that can be up to ten years in duration – a depth of skill that is relevant to a very wide client base, supervised experience in working with disturbed clients and an extensive understanding of how to deal with challenging situations such as suicidal ideation. If you are a coach without clinical or psychotherapeutic qualifications the section below will help you to understand more about these issues and what you can do to stay within the limits of your professional competence.

Education for clinical psychologists, counsellors and psychotherapists

While education for clinical psychologists varies in different districts and countries, students will typically complete a 3- or 4-year Bachelor's degree in psychology, some will then move onto a 2- to 4-year Master's degree then to a Doctorate in Clinical Psychology. To enter the doctoral programme, students will need a high grade in their previous degree. The doctoral programme is often a three-year, full-time course where trainees spend three days a week on supervised clinical practice placements and two days a week are dedicated to teaching, study and research. Completion of the degree will allow the individual to apply for registration or accreditation to a national professional body. Clinical psychology courses typically adhere to the reflective scientist-practitioner model with its emphasis on the integration of theory, research and practice in all aspects of the programme. They often have a broad psychosocial framework that identifies how biological, psychological and social factors contribute to the development and maintenance of psychological difficulties. Many programmes use the cognitive-behavioural therapy approach as the primary focus because of its strong evidence base. An example is the programme offered by King's College London: www.kcl.ac.uk/study/postgradua te-research/areas/doctorate-in-clinical-psychology-dclinpsy.

Psychotherapy and counselling education requirements also vary widely but a typical programme is a part time Master's degree with a clinical placement. Entry usually requires a 3- or 4-year degree in psychology, social sciences or related subject with a strong grade. This placement could require a minimum of 100 hours of client work during the programme and this would count towards the 450 hours often needed for registration as a psychotherapist or counsellor. An example of this type of programme is the University of Warwick: https://wa rwick.ac.uk/study/postgraduate/courses/msc-psychotherapy-counselling

These requirements mean that clinical psychology, counselling and psychotherapy are strongly regulated in most countries which contrasts with coaching, which is generally an unregulated profession.

The breadth of specialist areas in clinical psychology

To illustrate the depth of issues that may be covered in clinical psychology training (Davey et al., 2021) and not addressed in most coaching training, the following list is set out below:

Children and families

- Childhood development: of importance in this area is understanding the basic psychological needs of children and how the family and related contexts impact the social development, emotional adjustment, and mental health status of children.
- Adolescents' adjustment: the significance of the impact of the family and other social forces on the development, emotional adjustment, and mental health status of adolescents.

Adults with psychological difficulties

- Depression and suicidal thinking: a mood disorder that may involve a sufferer describing problems of sadness, loss, or anger that disrupts the person's well-being and everyday life. It may involve suicidal thoughts or ruminations about the possibility of committing suicide.
- Anxiety and panic disorders: which frequently involve intense, disproportionate, and persistent worry about everyday situations.
- Psychoses: these are severe mental health disorders associated with abnormal thinking and perceptions. They include psychotic disorders in which individuals can lose touch with reality with some experiencing delusions and hallucinations.
- Personality disorders: these can involve a lifelong condition where individuals have difficulties understanding emotions and tolerating distress. Their often impulsive behaviour means they struggle to relate to others socially, vocationally and so impacting their overall quality of life.
- Eating disorders: these are serious conditions that impact both physical and mental health and include problems with thinking about food, eating, weight and shape.
- Trauma: these involve problems triggered by a terrifying event that the person either experiences or witnesses and often involve flashbacks, nightmares, severe anxiety, and uncontrollable thoughts about the trauma.
- Forensic psychology involves working with adults or adolescents who have been involved in antisocial or criminal behaviour. It may include assessment, treatment and management of antisocial behaviour, as well as court assessments of individuals.

People with disabilities and physical challenges

- Intellectual disabilities: which involves an individual having difficulties concentrating, understanding, learning, and remembering new everyday events or objects.
- Autistic issues: a condition related to brain development that affects the way an individual perceives and socialises. It can cause different and sometimes problematic social interaction and communication. Individuals with this condition can also have a range of strengths for example the ability to memorise and learn complex information quickly.
- Physical illness and problems: working with individuals whose illness impacts their sense of self, their ability to adjust, resilience and how they find purpose and benefit in life.
- Dementia: working with people who are often older and are impacted by a group of symptoms affecting memory, thinking and social abilities.
- Neuropsychology: which examines the impact of brain injury or illness on cognitive processes, social development, physical functioning and emotional development.

What to do if you are not clinically trained

If you are not trained in clinical or counselling psychology or psychotherapy it does not mean that the advanced techniques in the book are off limits. It does mean that you need to be careful and thoughtful in proceeding. I recommend the following steps if you are a trained, supervised and ethically adherent coach:

1 Read as much as you can about the advanced approach you are interested in, starting with the chapters in this book and then moving on to the recommended readings set out at the end of each chapter. Find everything else you can about the technique examining the range of relevant books and articles in the area.
2 Discuss your interest and reading with your coaching supervisor and get their view on whether you should proceed further or not.
3 Find a training programme in the area of interest that is run by a reputable organisation or individual. Undertake the training and learn as much as you can.
4 Find a suitably qualified and registered clinical or counselling psychologist or psychotherapist who specialises in the area you are considering.
5 Undertake a period – say six months – of personal therapy to work on your own challenges and issues. Be clear with your therapist about your interest in the technique and see if it is possible to use this approach several times in your own personal therapy.
6 Check that this therapist is willing to supervise you in the use of the advanced technique in your own coaching practice. If your therapist

agrees you can start to look at your coaching case load and see if the use of the advanced technique is relevant.

7   Before using the approach with any client be very honest and direct about your interest but lack of experience with the technique. Check that the client is comfortable in proceeding at this point.

8   Undertake a client risk analysis by carefully checking if you can identify any potential psychological or social dangers in proceeding. Ask both your coaching supervisor and your therapist about their recommended approach in this area. In general terms, be sure that your client fits within the coaching population – that is, they have a reasonable degree of psychological, social and vocational stability.

9   Proceed carefully to use the approach with a willing and informed client. Be meticulous in monitoring for signs of distress or concern and immediately stop the approach if your client is not comfortable.

10 Discuss the session with both your coaching supervisor and therapist. Take their feedback seriously and learn any lessons arising from the situation.

Case study: a clinically trained coach

To illustrate the training of a coach who undertook clinical training, I present my own situation. I am from a middle-class family background in New Zealand. My father was a scientist with the Institute of Nuclear Sciences and my mother an entrepreneur who at one point ran three retail stores and looked after the family. I followed in my family footsteps by studying the physical sciences at university. However, I quickly found that this was not for me and in my second year failed all my courses. About this time, I went to a guest lecture given by Professor Tony Taylor on psychology and decided immediately that this is what I wanted to study. I eventually gained a Bachelor of Science degree in psychology, then after a year in social work, I did a Master of Social Science in psychology and a Diploma in Clinical Psychology. My Master's thesis involved a single case study of a client learning social skills. The Diploma involved a year of full-time supervised clinical work plus additional study. After completing my clinical qualification, I worked as a forensic clinical psychologist for some years in both men's and women's prisons as well as having a private clinical practice. While I was working in the forensic area, I was approached by Tony Taylor and asked if I wanted to be a field psychologist and researcher in an expedition to Antarctica. I went on this 70-day traverse into the high plateau of Antarctica and wrote my research work up as a Doctorate in work stress in extreme environments. I then worked in a consulting firm in New Zealand, Canada and Hong Kong for some years leading a team of management consultants. During this time my interest in coaching grew rapidly as it offered me the opportunity to use both my clinical and organisational psychology skills. I undertook coach training with Tony Grant and Michael Cavanagh from the University of Sydney. I started the Executive Coaching Centre in Auckland, New Zealand in 2000 and have been working in this area ever since. I have had an enduring interest in clinical psychology, have read this literature extensively over the years and now have a great interest in helping coaches use a wide range of evidence-based approaches to assist their clients.

Reflective practice exercise: Assess your coaching training

Write a brief paragraph on your education in general and your training as a coach.

Consider each of the following areas and decide if you have been trained in these. Rate your training, from 0 = Not at All; to 10 = Extensive training at a recognise tertiary education establishment.

Children and families

- Childhood development
- Adolescent adjustment

Adults with psychological difficulties

- Depression and suicidal thinking
- Anxiety and panic disorders
- Personality disorders
- Eating disorders
- Trauma
- Forensic psychology

People with disabilities and physical challenges

- Intellectual disabilities
- Autistic issues
- Physical illness and problems
- Dementia
- Neuropsychology

Describe the main topics in your coach training.

How has your training been different from that of a clinical psychologist?

Do you intent to start to use some of the advanced techniques outlined in this book? Is so how will you proceed?

Key learning points

- The advanced techniques in this book are more complex and therefore primarily recommended for those coaches who have completed clinical psychology, counselling or psychotherapy qualifications.

- The chapter outlines a range of typical topics covered in clinical psychology training and asks readers to compare their training to someone who undertook a clinical psychology education.
- There are steps that any trained, supervised and ethical coach can take to use these advanced techniques which include undertaking your own personal therapy with a suitably qualified professional so you can experience the approach from the client's perspective.

Discussion topics

Discuss someone that you may know or have met who is a clinical psychologist, counsellor, or psychotherapist. How is this person's language and approach different from you as a coach?

Discuss any personal therapy you have undertaken, the nature of this work and what you learned from it. Did this therapy provide you with some useful insights that you have been able to apply in your coaching?

Selected readings

Davey, G., Lake, N. & Whittington, A. (Eds). (2020). *Clinical psychology*. Routledge.

Holmes, J. & Storr, A. (2023). *The Art of Psychotherapy*. Taylor & Francis.

Linden, W. & Hewitt, P. L. (2015). *Clinical psychology: A modern health profession*. Psychology Press.

Palmer, S. & McMahon, G. (Eds). (1997). *Handbook of counselling*. Psychology Press.

Chapter 11

Imagery rescripting

This chapter introduces the idea that early painful memories have either a positive or negative impact on later life and so psychotherapies such as schema therapy have developed ways to help clients to alter or reframe early memories. One approach is imagery rescripting and this chapter describes the background to this approach. Imagery rescripting is an advanced technique that has clear origins in psychodynamic therapy because it places a strong emphasis on exploring painful memories from childhood. However, unlike much psychodynamic therapy which involves talking about and gaining insights into the past, imagery rescripting is an active form of therapy that aims to reframe or rewrite early memories. This chapter contains detailed instructions on how to implement this technique and a case study to illustrate the application. It includes typical comments from clients after using imagery rescripting, the key learning points from the chapter, a self-reflective exercise for readers plus discussion topics and further suggested reading.

Introduction to painful memories

Psychologists and philosophers have long been interested in how painful memories develop and then impact individuals later in life. They have asked a range of questions about these memories. How does early pain affect our subsequent pain experiences? Does early pain generate later chronic feelings of distress? How can these early pain memories be impacted or changed? We know that during early childhood cognitive or thinking skills develop rapidly at both a physiological and psychological level. Early in life children develop explicit memories of events and understand that these things have happened to them. They develop a sense of their thinking self which includes the way in which memories are organised and stored. Their developing language ability enables them to tell their own stories to others and this can help build memory retention (Noel et al., 2015).

Given the impact of early painful memories on later life, psychotherapies such as schema therapy have developed ways to help clients to alter or reframe these early memories.

DOI: 10.4324/9781003501824-11

Imagery rescripting in schema therapy

Schema therapy is an integrative approach that draws on methods and techniques from a range of areas including psychodynamic, cognitive behavioural, and gestalt therapy (Roediger et al., 2018).

Psychodynamic therapy is based on the work of Sigmund Freud and is a form of talking therapy derived from the principles of psychoanalysis (Jones, 1949). This type of therapy assumes that talking about problems helps people to address them and it places a strong emphasis on the client's early childhood and the impact of their memories on their well-being. It differs from other types of therapy because it focuses on understanding, expressing and overcoming painful, negative and often repressed feelings from childhood. It helps clients understand the origin of their problems and the impact of early experiences on their subsequent thinking, emotion and behaviour.

Imagery rescripting is an advanced schema therapy technique and should only be used by suitably qualified, trained, supervised and ethically adherent coaches. It is a central schema technique and has clear origins in psychodynamic therapy because it places a strong emphasis on early core painful memories from childhood. However, unlike psychodynamic therapy which involves talking about and gaining an understanding of the past, imagery rescripting is an active form of therapy that aims to reframe or rewrite early memories. It is an imagery-focused method that aims to reduce distressing memories or images and so to change the client's unhelpful beliefs about themselves. This technique has been successfully employed with a range of problems such as depression, eating disorders, obsessive compulsive disorder, social anxiety and posttraumatic stress disorder (Arntz, 2012).

Schema coaching uses schema therapy techniques, including imagery rescripting, but applies these to the challenges of high-functioning individuals in the workplace (McCormick, 2022). Imagery rescripting is only ever undertaken after a careful analysis of the background of the client, a risk assessment and then making a joint decision with the client that schema coaching is relevant and then educating the client about the approach. The technique involves the coach asking the client to think and talk about an early childhood memory that seems to be at the heart of the problematic schema that they suffer from. For example, a client with a pessimism schema may have many vivid memories of being told that they were hopeless by both parents and teachers. The client is then asked to close their eyes and repeat the story in the first person present 'I am now a six year old boy playing ball in the park and suddenly Mum laughs at me because I cannot catch the ball …' The coach does not guide the client's story in any way but does encourage the client to recall as much detail as possible. For example, 'What time of day were you in the park?' and 'What were you wearing?' Just before the emotional peak of the story the coach asks the client if they can come into the story and talk to the important players in the memory. The coach intervenes in the story and changes the painful situation in a way that greatly improves the ending and addresses the client's unmet need (McCormick, in press).

Imagery rescripting guidelines

Imagery rescripting guidelines to rewrite painful memories are set out below:

Step 1: Coach's instructions

1   As the coach, ensure that you have a deep understanding of the client's background, risk factors and that schema coaching is directly relevant to their needs.
2   Conduct a careful and thorough case conceptualisation to ensure that you have a deep understanding of the origin, current status and maintenance drivers of the challenge.
3   Discuss the schema model and the importance of imagery in schema coaching and gain consent to undertake this technique. Ensure that there is a high level of trust with the client and that they feel safe.
4   Ask the client to think about and then talk about an early childhood memory that seems to be at the heart of their schema.
5   Request the client to imagine the childhood event in as much detail as possible.
6   Then ask the client to close their eyes and tell the story in the first person present – 'I am now an eight year old girl ...'
7   Work with the client to form a clear image with as much detail as possible: 'What is happening, what do you see (hear, smell)? Why do you feel this way?' 'What happens next?' 'What are your feelings now?' 'What are you thinking?' What would help at this moment?'.

Step 2: Coach rescripts

1   The coach asks if they can enter the imagined scene at a point shortly before the emotional climax. It is important that if the scene is traumatic to the client that the coach intervenes at a point which stops the client being re-traumatised.
2   The coach enters the scene and talks to the client and the relevant others in turn in a way that addresses the client's unmet needs. For example, the coach may use a stern voice and stand up to a perpetrator, telling the client that they now have nothing to fear or that they are a good child and have nothing to be ashamed of. It is important that the coach projects confidence and emotion when making the intervention.
3   The coach then asks how the perpetrator responds and continues to meet the client's needs in whatever way is helpful. Perhaps taking them to an imaginary park to play or asking them to be in the football team.

4   Check how the client feels about the situation and address any remaining issues. For example, the client's father may give her a hug and tell her that he is very proud of her.
5   Check if there is anything else that the client needs.
6   When finished, ask the client to delete the scene from their mind and slowly come back to the present moment.

Step 3: Client debrief

1   Give the client the opportunity to recover from what is typically a very intense experience.
2   Ask the client what they saw, heard, felt, smelled, thought, etc. during the rescripting experience.
3   Then ask the client to step into the *healthy adult* mode, which is to use their mature executive functions, and ask what they experienced during the rescripting from this very different perspective.
4   Gently ensure that the client stays in a positive and more objective mode. Help the client to learn from the experience and to be able to draw on the powerful intervention whenever they need.
5   Check if this work has tired the client or if they want to push on to the next stage in this session. If the client is tired, move on to the Learning the Lessons step. However, if the client is ready, move to Step 4.

Step 4: Client self-rescripting

1   Ask if the client wants to become their own rescripting coach?
2   If they want to do this, ask them to re-enter another core childhood scene and describe the situation in detail and in the first person present.
3   Just before the emotional climax, ask the client to take on the role of the *healthy adult* and address the situation in a way that meets their needs. They may call the police, disarm a perpetrator, give themselves an ice cream, have a friend invite them to join a team and so on.
4   Ask the client if they are satisfied with the outcome and add extra components if they are not. Work on the scene until the client feels that their need has been met.
5   When ready, ask the client to delete the scene and slowly come back to the present moment.
6   Undertake the Client debrief as in Step 3 above.

Step 5: Learning the lessons

1   Take the time to congratulate the client on their courage in facing the scene and on their persistence to work through it.

2   If relevant, develop an action plan that suits the client to extend the range of scenes that need to be dealt with, based on the schema case conceptualisation.

Step 6: Follow-up

1   In the next session, ask how the client has implemented their action plan and assist in any way needed to help them make the most of the imagery rescripting.
2   Follow up after three months or when relevant and check that the client has been able to maintain the improvements gained by using imagery rescripting.

Key issues when using imagery rescripting

There is clear evidence that imagery can be effectively used to access emotions and so produce a unique way of enabling personal change. Imagery approaches have been shown to have a greater beneficial impact on both positive and negative emotions than simply talking about a situation. This is important as there is a strong relationship between disturbing 'unwanted' images and psychological distress. This is clearly seen in post-traumatic stress disorder but is also relevant in a wide range of other psychological challenges. Working with and altering images including the sense of touch, smell and sound can be highly beneficial for clients (Simpson & Arntz, 2020).

Generating the emotional response

It is important in imagery rescripting that the client is given sufficient time to get 'into' the imagined scene and experience it as fully as possible. By sensitively asking questions about what the client is seeing, hearing, smelling and feeling, the coach can help build up a fuller picture of a past event. I am often surprised by clients who start with only a vague picture of a difficult past event but when the imagery rescripting has started, they are then able to recall a great deal of detail such as the size and shape of the room they are in, the furniture, what they were wearing, the time of day, the season of the year and so on.

Several 'hotspots'

Difficult early memories often include several interconnected important events. For example, a client may remember feeling rejected by a parent, going to bed, then getting up and trying to talk to the parent about how they felt and finally going back to bed frustrated and dejected. In imagery rescripting it may be necessary to have all these linked events in the rescript for the client to feel that their unmet childhood needs were addressed. Careful sensitive listening to the client is critical to ensure that all 'hotspots' are identified and then addressed.

Addressing the protagonist and the situation

Imagery rescripting will only work if the coach rescripts in a way that enables the client to overcome the odds and 'win'. This may mean that the coach needs to tell the client they are very large and strong, that they have called the police or whatever it takes to ensure a positive outcome. Often telling the 'child' that they are not to blame and are 'good' is important to restoring a sense of well-being for the client. Asking the client if they are satisfied with the outcome of the scene can be critical, and continuing the rescripting until they are satisfied can be important.

Client driven rescripting

In the early stages of rescripting, it is the coach who is the intervening figure. However, given the right encouragement, time and support the intervention can come from an imagined 'hero' or other supportive individual generated by the client but acted out by the coach. With further practice the client can start to drive their own rescripting, acting out all roles, and using their *healthy adult* mode (the person's mature executive functions) to change the scene and support their own self-confidence and compassion.

Strengthening future change

Imagery rescripting can not only be effective in dealing with past painful events, but it is often helpful in increasing the likelihood of future adaptive behaviour and positive coping. For example, a client with a pessimism schema may be encouraged to use imagery to help them see themselves succeeding, whether it is in simply telling a funny joke or enjoying dancing. For executives, important scenes may include giving inspirational speeches or gaining agreement during a negotiation. In many cases, the imagery work needs to be supplemented by skills training to ensure success.

Building positive playful schema

Imagery techniques are very adaptable and can be used for assessment (exploring early events to identify schema), dealing with painful memories (by changing the ending of the scene into a positive coping image), strengthening coping (practicing future events and positive responses to them) and building positive playful schema. The latter can be done by practicing past, present or future events and ensuring that the imagery is life affirming and builds positive playful schema. For example, a client practising dealing with a highly critical client and finding a playful way of joking about the situation rather than allowing it to trigger early maladaptive schema.

Case study: Imagery rescripting

Amanda was a highly intelligent and capable accountant in an audit firm. She came to coaching to address her stress and anxiety. This involved regular feelings of worry and sleeplessness. She said that she had suffered from stress and anxiety since she was young and it had seriously hindered her enjoyment of life and her ability to form romantic relationships.

The case conceptualisation revealed that she had a passive father and an abusive mother who suffered from mental health issues. Her core childhood memory was of her mother coming home from work, walking into Amanda's bedroom when she was taking a break from doing her homework and yelling at her for being 'slack and lazy'. The sudden and unexpected nature of the verbal attack had left Amanda deeply shocked and scared.

The first three sessions with Amanda involved solution-focused coaching, but little headway was made. So, the coach discussed the nature of schema coaching and in particular imagery rescripting as a means of re-writing memories, and Amanda said she was very interested in trying the approach.

In an extended two hour session the coach asked her to tell the story of her mother's verbal abuse in the first person present – 'I am now a nine year old girl …'. The coach encouraged her to develop a clear image with as much detail as possible by asking Amanda to describe her bedroom, her desk, what she was wearing, what her mother was wearing and what she saw, heard, smelled and felt.

Just at the point in the story where her mother burst into the room the coach asked if he could intervene and after Amanda agreed he said in a stern loud voice to her mother – 'Now you just wait right there – Amanda is just taking a break from her homework, she is a good girl and yelling at her will terrify her!'. The coach then turned to Amanda and said 'Do not worry. I will protect you from this. I will tell your mother to go away and calm down. She will now go and have a cup of tea and come back and talk to you sensibly'. The coach then asked, 'How does that feel Amanda?'. Amanda said that felt good but she was not sure that her mother would leave the room. The coach again termed to the mother and said sternly 'Leave the room now. Right now. Good. Please close the door, have a cup of tea, calm down and come back and only talk to Amanda when you are able to be sensible'. The coach turned to Amanda and said, 'She has left the room now, how does that feel?'. Amanda said, 'That feels great, that feels brilliant, I can see that she has gone now!'.

The coach gave Amanda a few minutes to calm down and then said when you are ready, please delete the scene from your mind, open your eyes and slowly come back to the present moment. The coach then asked Amanda how she felt and Amanda said 'I feel strangely empowered by your stern voice telling my mother to stop abusing me, and this is now permanently engraved in my brain. Thank you for that'.

Amanda went on to practice imagery rescripting as part of her schema coaching homework and worked on a whole range of painful memories from her childhood. After three months coaching, she said 'I am feeling a lot stronger now, somehow the volume of the demons in my head has greatly reduced. I still get anxious from time to time but now I feel I can make better sense of it and I can deal with it'. She said that her enjoyment of life had greatly improve and that she had started a romantic relationship.

Client feedback

The following are a summary of typical comments made by clients about using imagery rescripting in schema coaching adapted from McCormick (in press).

QUESTION: What is imagery rescripting?

CLIENT RESPONSE: It is a process that is used to rewrite what you experienced as a child that had a lasting impact on you. It is about changing a difficult memory, because you are stuck in the old story and this is holding you back from enjoying life.

QUESTION: Why did you undertake imagery rescripting as part of your schema coaching?

CLIENT RESPONSE: I used it because I felt really stuck in the past by painful things that had happened to me, and I wanted to get that stuff out of my head and into the rubbish bin.

QUESTION: What were your positive and negative experiences with imagery rescripting?

CLIENT RESPONSE: It was a positive experience overall if very challenging. It gave me a safe space to think deeply and to experience something entirely different. It was painful to think about the situation but very powerful and healing.

QUESTION: What was helpful or less helpful about the behaviour of the coach?

CLIENT RESPONSE: The introduction that the coach gave was very clear and it helped me to understand what was coming. The event was very powerful and I was totally absorbed. I was very strongly supported by the coach throughout the experience. It was a very different experience but I did feel safe, which was essential.

QUESTION: What was the impact of imagery rescripting?

CLIENT RESPONSE: In the short term, I was drained and exhausted. I felt lucky that I did not have to go back to work immediately after the session. I went for a drive, stopped by the sea and just let the whole experience wash over me. I had time to digest it. Since then, I have thought about it many times and it has helped me get the most out of the experience. Over the longer term I have felt calmer and during the months since the session I have thought a lot more about the events and how I can re-interpret them. The greatest impact came from hearing the voice of the coach with the power and emotion that was put into it.

QUESTION: What did you learn from doing imagery rescripting?

CLIENT RESPONSE: I have come to understand the power of early childhood experiences and how they impact you in a very subtle but forceful way. I learned it is a real challenge to directly experience the painful past. I also learned that you can manage your memories and recreate them. I now know how to revisit the past and imbue it with love and compassion.

QUESTION: Would you recommend imagery rescripting to others?

CLIENT RESPONSE: Yes absolutely. I meet a lot of distressed individuals who have deep challenges and these people could really benefit from this approach.

QUESTION: What are your comments for other coaches who use imagery rescripting?

CLIENT RESPONSE: This is a very powerful technique, so the coach needs to be well trained and highly competent. It is an advanced approach that is highly effective in the right hands.

Tips for coaches

- During the rescripting process ensure that you encourage the client to stay in the first person present (I am now ...), particularly as they enter the scene. Gentle correction is particularly important at the start of the imagining to get the client on the best path (It is best if you continue with ... I am now ...). If the client starts talking in the past tense and in the third person (I can remember that we ...), the impact can easily be lost.
- Not being able to find the 'right' scene. Sometimes the client is unable to decide which scene to use in the rescripting and spends a long time deciding on the 'right' one. Under these circumstances it is often best to explain to the client that there is no correct or best scene and that they will be able to work on a range of scenes over time if they wish. Beginning with the clearest and most vivid scene can be a useful starting point.
- Not starting with a highly traumatic scene. If the person asks about using a particularly traumatic scene in initial rescripting explain that it can be best to begin with a midlevel intensity scene and to ensure the client understands the importance of intervening before the climax of the scene to avoid re-traumatisation. When this point is understood, progress can be made to higher-intensity scenes.
- The right balance between motivating tension but not overwhelm is vital in imagery rescripting. Working to ensure that the client has a healthy level of emotional regulation is vital. Should the client not be able to

engage strongly with the scene, asking them about the details involved can be very important (Was it a sunny day? Which room were you in?). However, if the client is emotionally volatile it can be very useful to start the process by getting them to focus on a safe scene. For example, watching a sunset and telling them they can return to this scene at any time if they feel overwhelmed during the imagery rescripting.

- Careful attention needs to be given to homework to ensure that the client does not try to rescript a traumatic early memory and retraumatise themselves. It can be useful to ask the client which scenes they would like to use in homework and to explicitly instruct them not to use traumatic scenes and explain the dangers of retraumatising themselves.

- Watch for dissociation which can range from a mild emotional detachment from the imagined scene (the details of the scene are starting to fade), to a more severe disconnection from physical and emotional reality (I feel lightheaded and am drifting away). If needed, the coach can ask the client to open their eyes, to give them a drink of water and suggest that they continue the rescripting when the client feels more ready to do so.

- Loyalty to the antagonist. Sometimes the client will feel conflicted during the rescripting when the coach is addressing the antagonist or sometimes the client will bring up the disloyalty issue in a follow up session. This can arise when the client has an early childhood memory of a cruel or abusive parent but now this person has changed and the client now feels warmth towards this aged and more mellowed individual. It can be useful for the coach to explain that the rescripting is about reshaping the story of the parent 'as they were back then'. Often this separation between the cruel early parent and the current loving parent can be extremely helpful and enable the client to understand and resolve their contradictory feelings about the person. This issue can also be helped by the coach being sensitive to it and having a firm yet compassionate approach to the antagonist ('Dad, I understand that you had a hard life, that you are angry and frustrated but hitting Jimmy is just unacceptable, you must stop right now').

Reflective practice exercise – imagery rescripting

The following exercise aims to help the reader to think more deeply about the topic and to consider applying the approach in their own practice.

As a coach who has been reading about imagery rescripting and how it is possible to re-write painful memories, what is the most important thing you have learned from this chapter?

Example: I learned about the amazing power that this technique can sometimes have.

What areas do you need to know more about?

> Example: I want to know more about what happens if the client's memory is poor and they cannot clearly imagine the scene.

What additional training will you explore?

> Example: I want to find a highly experiential training course in this area.

What elements of imagery rescripting do you feel most confident about? What areas are you least confident about?

> Example: I feel confident about explaining the technique to a client and least confident about actually intervening in the memory.

What topics will you discuss with your supervisor?

> Example: I will discuss how I can get started in this, without getting outside my area of competence.

Do you plan to undertake some imagery rescripting to deal with your own personal issues and how will you arrange this?

> Example: Yes, I, like everyone, have some skeletons that I need to deal with. It is a wonderful opportunity to get to know myself better. I will find a capable schema therapist to work with.

Post-imagery rescripting reflective practice exercise

The following exercise aims to help the reader to reflect on their use of imagery rescripting in their own coaching practice.

Describe the imagery rescripting exercise that you have just undertaken.

> Example: I was working with a senior executive with a failure schema and we used imagery rescripting to address an early painful school memory.

What did you feel as you were undertaking the work with the client?

> Example: This is the first time I have used imagery rescripting with a client and I was very nervous. However, I pushed on into it and tried not to display any uncertainty.

How would you evaluate the experience? What was good and bad?

Example: As I said, I was nervous to start but became more confident as we progressed. I was able to confront a bully at school who was bothering the client and the bully backed off.

What did you learn from the situation?

Example: I learned that imagery rescripting is very powerful but taxing for the client. I learned that despite my worry, I can successfully use this approach.

What would I do differently next time?

Example: Next time I would ask the client to identify their core childhood memory and understand it in depth, then in the next session I would do the rescripting. In this way I could practice options more and be more confident.

Key learning points

1   Given the impact of early painful memories on later life, schema therapy has developed ways to alter or reframe early memories. One relevant schema technique is called imagery rescripting.
2   It is a method that aims to reduce distressing memories or images and so to change the client's unhelpful beliefs about themselves. It has been successfully used with a range of problems such as depression, eating disorders, obsessive compulsive disorder, social anxiety and posttraumatic stress disorder.
3   The technique is very impactful and should only be used by fully trained, experienced, supervised and ethically adherent coaches.
4   The technique involves the coach asking the client to think and talk about an early childhood memory that seems to be at the heart of their problematic schema. The client is then asked to close their eyes and repeat the story in the first person present 'I am now a six year old boy ...'. Just before the emotional peak of the story, the coach asks the client if they can come into the story and talk to the important players in the memory. The coach intervenes in the story and changes the painful situation in a way that greatly improves the ending and addresses the client's unmet need.
5   Clients generally find imagery rescripting very helpful. In the short term it is draining even exhausting. However, over the longer term, clients typically feel calmer and more at peace with themselves.

Discussion topics

Consider your current coaching client base and discuss which clients may benefit from imagery rescripting. Why did you choose these clients?

If you wish to use any of the advanced schema techniques in this book, it is strongly recommended that you first find a schema therapist and work on some of your own issues using the schema approach. Discuss how you may find a schema therapist that you can contact and possibly work with.

Selected readings

Arntz, A. (2012). Imagery rescripting as a therapeutic technique: Review of clinical trials, basic studies, and research agenda. *Journal of Experimental Psychopathology*, 3(2), 189–208.

McCormick, I. A. (in press). Schema coaching techniques, part 3: Imagery rescripting and transformational chairwork. In *The Coaching Psychologist*.

Roediger, E., Stevens, B. A. & Brockman, R. (2018). *Contextual Schema Therapy: An integrative approach to personality disorders, emotional dysregulation, and interpersonal functioning*. New Harbinger Publications.

Simpson, S. & Arntz, A. (2020). Core principles of imagery. In Heath, G. & Startup, H. (Eds). *Creative methods in Schema therapy: advances and innovation in clinical practice*. Routledge.

Chapter 12

Chairwork and other dialogue techniques

This chapter explains how coaches can help clients understand their inner dialogue, mood changes and the impact of these on their well-being. It examines the nature of the inner dialogue, provides background to an important schema technique, chairwork and sets out detailed instructions on how this approach can be used. Chairwork is a collective term for a broad range of approaches used to assist clients to understand and better deal with their own inner conversations. These approaches all involve the use of chairs to help clients to separate the different parts of themselves in the present moment. Other related dialogue techniques include the talking-back diary which involves asking the client to write down their inner critic thoughts on one side of a page. Having written down a range of critical thoughts the client is asked to try to create a healthy adult response to each of these. This exercise helps the client to better understand the nature of their inner conflict between critic and healthy adult. The chapter also includes an illustrative case study, a reflective practice exercise, key learning points, discussion topics and suggested further reading.

The inner dialogue

William James (1890) the famous philosopher and psychologist was probably the first person to run a psychology course in the United States. James wrote extensively in psychology and pointed out that during personal introspection our sense of self can become split into two parts, firstly the Me or myself (self-as-known) and secondly the I or the observing self (self-as-knower). Most of us are aware of these different parts of ourselves and the resulting inner dialogue that provides an ongoing commentary on our lives every day. This self-talk is a combination of conscious thoughts and unconscious values and biases, that can often be supportive or negative and unhelpful. There are a wide range of techniques that can be used to help clients change the nature of their inner dialogue (Roediger et al., 2018).

DOI: 10.4324/9781003501824-12

Chairwork

Chairwork is a collective term for a broad range of approaches used to assist clients to understand and better deal with their own inner dialogue. These approaches all involve the use of chairs to help clients to separate the different parts of themselves in the present moment. For example, a coach may notice the critical tone that a client uses to comment on their own recent failure. The coach could then arrange two chairs and ask the client to sit in one and be the critical self and talk to the person as-usual-self using this harsh tone. The coach could ask the client to change chairs and talk back to the critical self explaining that this tone is not helpful. This could then be expanded into a fuller dialogue which helps the client build awareness and choice.

Chairwork was first used by Jacob L. Moreno, a Romanian-American psychiatrist, psychosociologist and educator, who was the founder of psychodrama (Moreno, 1946). Psychodrama is an active form of group psychotherapy that offers a creative way to explore and address personal challenges. In psychodrama clients act out situations so they can better personally understand and gain insights into these. The members of the group who assist in the role playing also often gain insights into their own lives by participating in the group drama.

It was Fritz Perls who popularised the chairwork approach in what he called gestalt therapy, which was developed with his wife, Laura Perls, in the 1940s. Chairwork is based on the central gestalt therapy process of building awareness and insight into bodily feelings, emotion, and behaviour, in the present moment (Perls, 1969). The approach is used in many ways, but one variation is for the client to sit in one chair and imagine a person that they have had a conflict with, in a second chair. The client speaks to the other person and frankly shares their feelings with them. Then the client moves chairs taking on the role of the other person and expresses their emotions from that perspective. This movement between chairs and roles enables the client to connect with both sides of the situation and to understand their struggle from a broader, more helpful perspective (Kellogg, 2015).

Both schema therapy and coaching use chairwork in a variety of ways to help clients address painful experiences and to reinforce the impact of the healthy adult. The approach can also be used to minimise the power of the inner critic and so to reduce self-loathing and derision (Roediger et al., 2018).

One important use of chairwork is to help the client understand schema modes or complex mood states. For example, the coach may arrange four chairs, one for the client, one for their inner critic, one for their angry child and the fourth for the healthy adult. The coach may then ask the client to explain a challenging mood state. After the client has done this the coach may ask them to sit in the inner critic chair and talk to themselves using the punitive language that typifies this critical mood state. This fault-finding dialogue may trigger anger in the client so the coach may ask the client to sit in the angry child chair and frankly express their feelings. Having explored these mood state changes the coach may ask the client to think about the situation from the perspective of the healthy adult and provide a rational perspective to themselves. This would be done when the client was sitting in the healthy adult chair. After exploring these viewpoints, the client may be asked to sit in the original chair and to reflect on the situation and what they have learned. This chairwork can be very effective in providing a broader easily comprehensible view of an entangled and previously confusing inner dialogue. It can help the client to argue with their inner critic and so reject the seemingly unchangeable self-condemnation that is often seen in clients (Roediger et al., 2018).

The effectiveness of gestalt therapy

Schema coaching is a recent development (McCormick, 2022) and so there is little research into the effectiveness of any of its techniques. However, for the evidence-focused coach insights can be gained by looking into the effectiveness of gestalt therapy as a whole.

In an investigation into the effectiveness of gestalt therapy and hypnosis González-Ramírez et al. (2017) selected 30 individuals from a total of 300 who were diagnosed with depression. The clients were allocated to three groups: hypnosis therapy, gestalt-hypnosis therapy and a control group. Before and after assessments indicated clients undergoing hypnosis therapy and gestalt-hypnosis therapy showed statistically significant improvements. The authors concluded that both therapies showed promise in treating depression in this Mexican sample.

In a systematic review of empirical evidence into the effectiveness of gestalt therapy, Raffagnino (2019) reviewed studies published in English and Italian between 2007 and 2018. The author found 1,215 related research papers and after assessing their methodological adequacy selected just 11 papers for further review. These papers involved research conducted in a wide range of countries including Australia, Iran, Italy, Mexico, Norway, Serbia and Spain. The majority of research studies used the simple pre-post design with group therapy and so produced a rudimentary evaluation of effectiveness. A sample of studies compared gestalt therapy with other therapeutic approaches such as cognitive behaviour therapy, psychodynamic therapy and person-centred therapy. They evaluated gestalt therapy with anxious parents of primary school children, divorced women, offenders with psychopathological symptoms and troubled indigenous native people. After considering the range of studies Raffagnino concluded that there was some initial evidence that gestalt was effective.

A meta-analysis of 86 studies on the effectiveness of humanistic therapies including gestalt therapy was undertaken by Elliott (2002). After the review the author concluded that clients who undertook humanistic therapies showed, on average, significant changes over time. They also found that gains post-therapy are stable. The author examined a range of randomised clinical trials using untreated controls and found that those who undertook humanistic therapies show substantially more change than these untreated controls. In studies that compared the use of humanistic therapies with non-humanistic therapies the results suggested that the levels of change were equivalent.

Although the effectiveness research to date is not strong, the evidence-based coach can cautiously proceed with gestalt therapy approaches in their work.

Other dialogue techniques

There are a wide range of other techniques used in schema coaching that encourage clients to articulate their inner dialogue to build understanding, awareness and choice.

The talking-back diary – this technique involves asking the client to write down their inner critic thoughts on one side of a page. Having written down a range of critical thoughts the client is asked to try to find a healthy adult response to each of these (Roediger et al., 2018). If the client feels stuck, the coach might ask them to think about what a wise friend might say to the critical thoughts. This approach can often be useful as a stepping stone to finding and strengthening the healthy adult response. If the client is still stuck, they may use this as a homework exercise and spend some time between sessions trying to slowly get in touch with their healthy adult responses. This talking-back diary exercise helps clients to better understand the nature and frequency of their inner critic and to realise that this inner voice is just one perspective and not the 'truth'. An example of a talking-back diary is given below.

The mood diary – this is a slightly more complex technique where the client observes their inner thoughts and emotions during the day and encourages themselves to get in touch with their healthy adult and act in ways that are positive and helpful. The diary consists of six columns: the time of day, the action that is planned, the inner voice or emotion at this point, the healthy adult response, the impact of this response, the lesson learned from doing this. An example of a mood diary is set out below (adapted from Roediger et al., 2018).

A blank form of the mood diary can be found in the Appendix.

Table 12.1 Dialogue between the inner critic and healthy adult

Inner critic voice	Healthy adult response
That was a fatal error you made	Everyone makes mistakes occasionally
I will never be able to complete this	I need to keep trying and see how I go
She really dislikes me	She may just be in a bad mood
You are a fool	You, like everyone else, stuffs things up from time to time

Table 12.2 An example of a mood diary

Time	Planned action	Inner voice or emotion	Healthy adult response	Impact	Lesson learned
6.30 am	Alarm sounds	I want more sleep now!	Snooze for 5 minutes	Feel better	Being gentle on myself is useful
7.00 am	Breakfast	Same old thing!	Tonight, I will plan a differ-ent breakfast	I look for-ward to tomorrow	Planning helps a lot
7.30 am	Travel	Boring!	I will listen to a podcast	Great story	Distraction from the inner critic is useful
8.30 am	Start work	This is too much – I am bored	Talk to a colleague	She is bored too	I am not alone in this
10.00 am	Coffee break	Good coffee	Enjoy	Feel good	Enjoy the moment

Case study: chairwork

Freya was a hard working young lawyer who was determined to make it into the partnership of the downtown law firm that she worked for. Her first few years at the firm had gone really well and she gained great performance ratings from the senior associate who was her team leader. However, last year Freya had been promoted to senior associate and now reported directly to Judy a rather blunt and insensitive partner. Freya tried hard to please Judy but somehow it just did not work. She found herself worrying about her career prospects and not sleeping well at nights. As part of the firm's well-being programme, she decided to see an executive coach. Freya talked to the coach about her sleep problems and how she had been trying to go to bed early every weeknight to make up for the last sleep. The coach asked her if she felt that this worked, and Freya said it had not. The coach introduced the idea of sleep restriction therapy and suggested that Freya initially reduce the amount of time that she spent in bed and then after some weeks, gradually increase that time. The coach explained that Freya had probably gotten into the bad habit of going to bed early but then lying awake for some hours in the middle of the night. If she went to bed half an hour later and got up half an hour earlier her body would learn that bed is just for sleeping, suggested the coach. In the next session two weeks later, Freya said that this approach had initially been very challenging but over time it worked well and that she was now sleeping much better. However, she explained that she still felt very anxious and concerned about her relationship with Judy and her long-term career prospects in the firm.

The coach asked her if she felt comfortable exploring some of the relationship dynamics with Judy and Freya said she would try anything. The coach and

Freya then had a long conversation about Judy, her team and how this division of the firm was performing. Freya said that she had recently come to understand that Judy was under considerable pressure from the firm's management because the work of the division had been bid at a low charge-out rate and that this resulted in the division failing to meet its profit targets. The coach then arranged four chairs and said to Freya that one would represent her critical self, one her healthy adult, one was Judy and the final one was the firm's management. The coach suggested that Freya sit in the critical self chair and talk through her worrying thoughts. Freya was a little shy at first but with encouragement from the coach she said, 'Freya you better wake your ideas up if you want to be a partner in the firm!'. Then the coach suggested she sit in the Judy chair and talk about what was going on. Freya said 'My division is in a really bad place at the moment, and I am stressed to the max. I have management on my case demanding that things change and it makes me very tense and abrupt'. The coach then asked Freya to play the role of management and talk to Judy. She said 'Judy you did well in gaining this large government assignment, but the way in which it was bid is causing real problems. The charge-out rates you used were too low, and now we have a profit crisis'. The coach then asked Freya to again sit in the Judy chair and respond. She said 'Yes, I accept that this happened but we are nearly at the end of the work and we will be able to use much more realistic charge-out rates in the next phase of the work. The client likes what we are doing and will not go out to tender for the next phase'. The coach then asked Freya to sit in the healthy adult chair and reflect on the conversation so far. Freya said 'Although I know what is going on for Judy, it really clarifies things to hear it out loud. Freya has been worrying about Judy's coldness but actually it is totally understandable, and it is in no way a reflection on Freya's performance'. The coach said, 'Now finally I want you to sit in the healthy adult chair and tell me how you feel'. Freya moved chairs and said, 'I feel so different now, I have been beating myself up for something that is not my fault and is something I have no control over'. 'What is the action plan coming out of our session today?' asked the coach. Freya said, 'Well, tomorrow I will find some time when Judy seems in a reasonable mood and ask her what I can do to help as I understand we are under some performance pressure from the firm's management'.

In the next session Freya reported that Judy had been extremely appreciative of her offer to help and even had a tear in her eye when she thanked Freya for her thoughtfulness. Freya said that the chairwork had really helped her to look at the situation through a totally different and very helpful lens.

Reflective practice exercise: Inner dialogue

Write down a challenge or difficulty that you have which involves an unhelpful inner dialogue. This can be any situation, at work, at home, etc.

Example: My diet has deteriorated over winter and I need to do something about it.

Identify the nature of the dialogue. Is this a conflict between your inner critic and healthy adult? Who are the voices in your head?

Example: My inner critic is on at me a lot to stop eating junk food. However, this only makes me more anxious and so more likely to do so.

Be sure that you include the perspective of the healthy adult in your practice even if this voice is weak or almost non-existent at the moment. This is important because the likely resolution of this inner conflict is to build on the logic and power of your healthy adult.

Example: I need to get in touch with my healthy adult as I can see how unhelpful my inner critic is.

Use the talking-back diary approach to examine in detail your inner dialogue. Write down your inner critic or other thoughts on one side of a page. Having written down a range of these critical thoughts, find a healthy adult response to each of these. If you feel stuck, try to think about what a wise friend might say to your critical or unhelpful thinking. Using this approach, spend time developing your healthy adult.

Example: When the inner critic says, 'Just stop eating junk right now!' The healthy adult can say 'Self-criticism is not helpful, why don't you just go out now and buy some fruit to eat when you are hungry?'

Develop and write down an action plan based on this exercise so that you can start to strengthen your healthy adult voice in a range of important areas in your life.

Example: Twice a week I will buy some fruit and leave it on my desk at work. I will recognise that this is a big step forward and use my healthy adult to emphasise this.

Key learning points

1   Most of us are aware of our inner dialogue that provides an ongoing commentary on our lives every day. This self-talk is a combination of conscious thoughts and unconscious values and biases, that can be supportive or negative and unhelpful. There are a wide range of techniques that can be used to help both you and your clients change the nature of this inner dialogue.

2   One evidence-based approach to understanding and managing the inner dialogue is the empty chair technique. The approach is used in many ways, but one variation is for the client to sit in one chair and imagine a person that they have had a conflict with in a second chair. The client speaks to the other person and frankly shares their feelings with them. Then the client moves chairs taking on the role of the other person and expresses their emotions from that perspective. This movement between chairs and roles enables the client to connect with both sides of the situation and to understand their struggle from a broader, more helpful perspective.

3   Other dialogue techniques include the talking-back diary which involves asking the client to write down their inner critic thoughts on one side of a page. Having written down a range of critical thoughts, the client is asked to try to find a healthy adult response to each of these. This exercise assists the client to better understand the nature or their inner dialogue and to build their healthy adult.

4   A related technique is the mood diary in which the client observes their inner thoughts and emotions during the day and encourages themselves to get in touch with their healthy adult and act in ways that are positive and helpful. The diary consists of six columns: the time of day, the action planned, the inner voice or emotion at this point, the healthy adult response, the impact of this response and the lesson learned from doing this.

Discussion topics

Consider your current coaching client base and discuss any possible clients that may benefit from chairwork or other dialogue techniques.

If you wanted to use the techniques in this chapter in your coaching work, but had no experience of these, discuss how you could obtain personal therapy so that you can better understand the approach from the client's perspective and improve your own well-being.

Discuss how you would use your current supervision arrangements to ensure that you stay within your areas of competence as you start to use these techniques.

Selected readings

Bluckert, P. (2020). *Gestalt Coaching: Distinctive Features*. Routledge.

Kellogg, S. (2014). *Transformational chairwork: Using psychotherapeutic dialogues in clinical practice*. Rowman & Littlefield.

Mann, D. (2020). *Gestalt therapy: 100 key points and techniques*. Routledge.

Perls, F.S. (1969). *Gestalt Therapy Verbatim*. Gestalt Journal Press.

Chapter 13

Emotional exposure

Schema coaching draws upon a wide range of proven therapeutic techniques that are relevant to clients at work. This chapter explains how clients typically try to avoid difficult or painful experiences and how this can make problems worse. It sets out detailed instructions on how to help clients expose themselves in a safe way to painful situations. There are four types of evidence-based exposure training: imagined exposure where the client uses their imagination to face the feared situation, in vivo exposure where the client faces the anxiety producing situation in real life, virtual reality exposure that uses technology to simulate fearful situations and interoceptive exposure that involves the client generating feared physical sensations and learning that these are harmless. There are a wide range of speeds in the rate of therapeutic exposure from flooding that involves rapid and intense exposure to the feared situation to systematic desensitisation which involves learning a form of relaxation and then using imagined exposure to a graduated hierarchy or ladder of fear. The chapter also includes an illustrative case study, a reflective practice exercise, key learning points, discussion topics and suggested further reading.

Introduction to emotional exposure

Schema coaching employs a variety of evidence-based therapeutic approaches that are relevant to workplace challenges (McCormick, 2022, 2023a) and this range of techniques includes emotional exposure. The American Psychological Association (APA, 2024) states that exposure therapy is an evidence-based approach that assists clients to confront their fears or other situations that they routinely avoid. Exposure treatment is based on the idea that avoiding painful or fearful situations reduces anxiety in the short term but in the long term it generates more. The short term reduction in anxiety and associated sense of relief can become a powerful reward thus strengthening the avoidance behaviour. Emotional exposure aims to provide a safe environment in which the client can face their fears or anxieties in a way that is not overwhelming or overly troublesome. In this way the client can learn to tolerate

DOI: 10.4324/9781003501824-13

mild levels of discomfort and stop the experiential avoidance that reinforces the fear and anxiety.

The American Psychological Association (APA, 2024) indicates that therapeutic exposure has a range of variants as summarised below:

- Imagined exposure: this variant entails the client using their imagination to face their feared situation or activity. For example, a client may have a fear of making a mistake which leads to lots of double checking of their work and so a low level of performance. This client may be asked to imagine finding a minor and inconsequential error in a piece of work and facing this fear. The client thus uses imagined situations to slowly face their anxieties and learn that the consequences of this are unpleasant but minor.
- In vivo exposure: this involves the client directly facing the anxiety producing situation in real life. For example, the client may be asked to leave a minor spelling error in a draft report and so face the possibility of criticism from others.
- Virtual reality exposure: this entails the client using technology to simulate situations and can be very useful when vivo exposure is impossible. For example, using virtual reality headsets to gain exposure to a wartime battle situation and learning to remain calm enough to behave rationally.
- Interoceptive exposure: this variant involves the client generating feared physical sensations and learning that these are harmless. For example, rapidly running on the spot for two minutes may lead to breathlessness and feelings of panic, yet with repeated practice the client can learn that while unpleasant this activity is harmless.

There are a wide range of speeds in the rate of exposure:

- Flooding involves rapid and intense exposure to the feared situation and works on the logic that this will quickly enable the client to see that what they fear is, in fact, not threatening. Clearly this needs to be used with caution otherwise the client will drop out of coaching. This can be useful for mildly conflict anxious clients where they may need to write a complaint email or return some goods to a retail outlet.
- Graded exposure that involves building a hierarchy or ladder of gradually increasing fear or discomfort intensity, then systematically exposing the clients to this. For example, speaking in front of a small group of friends, then a small group of strangers, a moderately sized mixed audience then a large group of strangers.
- Systematic desensitization that involves learning a form of relaxation such as deep muscle relaxation and then using imagined exposure to a graduated hierarchy or ladder of fear. This sort of exposure can be useful when the client has stronger fears and where flooding would be unacceptable to them. For example, a coach who has a frighteningly

outspoken client whom they want to maintain a relationship with and so need to gradually learn to be calmer when interacting with them.

Clients can benefit from exposure therapy in a range of ways:

1   Extinction: which means that the level of learned emotional intensity deceases over time as a result of repeated contact.
2   Habituation: where clients come to understand that the fear will never lead to catastrophic outcomes.
3   Self-efficacy: where they learn to be confident that they can deal with fearful situations and that the outcomes are trivial.
4   Emotional processing: they come to change their beliefs about the feared activities and reframe them. For example, a coaching client may come to see that their verbally aggressive boss is actually under pressure themselves and start to feel sorry for them rather than fearful of them.

Given the large range of variants of emotional exposure, the coach needs to undertake a careful case conceptualisation so that they have a clear understanding of the client's emotional tolerance and level of desire for the speed of the resolution of the issue. The coach also needs to help the client understand the purpose and function of the fear so the client can make sense of it. It is also useful for the coach to explain why a particular exposure variant has been chosen, why and how it works and steps the client can take to move into a healthy adult frame of reference (Roediger et al., 2018).

Exposure therapy effectiveness

There has been a great deal of research on the effectiveness of exposure therapy and a small sample of that is presented below so that any schema coach can feel a degree of confidence that they are using an evidence-based approach.

In a study on the impact of prolonged exposure therapy in veterans diagnosed with post-traumatic stress disorder (PTSD), Eftekhari et al. (2013) had 1,931 veterans complete a 4-day prolonged exposure workshop. The authors found that there were significant reductions in symptoms of PTSD for both men and women no matter which war era they served in. Their conclusion was that for the veteran's population, prolonged exposure was effective in reducing the impact of PTSD and depression.

A meta-analysis was undertaken to compare the impact of virtual reality exposure therapy and traditional cognitive behavioural exposure therapy (DiMauro, 2014). The author examined 26 studies and found a greater impact from traditional exposure therapy than virtual reality exposure with these military clients showing lower posttreatment PTSD symptoms.

Lely et al. (2019) evaluated the impact of narrative exposure therapy with traumatised refugees and other trauma survivors. This type of exposure therapy used the writing of trauma-based stories as an exposure method of assisting clients with PTSD. The authors assessed 16 randomised-controlled trials (947 participants) and found significant reductions for PTSD symptoms at post-treatment and follow-up. The studies produced large positive effect sizes. Depression symptoms also reduced at post-treatment and follow-up with medium positive effect sizes being found. They concluded that exposure therapy was more effective than both other trauma-focused treatments and non-active controls. They suggested that therapy providers and clients alike can expect that exposure therapy will produce sustained treatment results.

In a systematic meta-analyses and review of the long-term impact of narrative exposure therapy for adults, children and trauma perpetrators, Siehl et al. (2021) examined 56 studies that compared 1,370 exposure treatment subjects to 1,055 controls from 30 countries. This review found that PTSD symptoms were significantly decreased when exposure therapy was compared with control conditions. The authors conclusion was that narrative exposure therapy can be effective for a wide range of traumatised clients who were living in challenging conditions.

In a 2022 study (McLean et al., 2022) used a meta-analysis to examine the impact of exposure therapy on clients diagnosed with PTSD as compared with control conditions. Their meta-analysis examined 934 studies with only 65 of these meeting their research quality criteria. With 4,929 patients they found that exposure therapy demonstrated significant decreases in symptoms as compared with waitlist and treatment-as-usual conditions. At follow up the positive effect sizes were stable and the review demonstrated that exposure had a greater impact than medication. The authors concluded that overall, exposure therapy was effective for the treatment of PTSD.

Morina et al. (2023) undertook a meta-analysis of virtual reality exposure therapy for social anxiety disorder using 12 studies, six of which were random controlled trials. They found that across all reports there were large pre-post and follow-up effect sizes. They concluded that virtual reality exposure therapy can significantly reduce symptom intensity for social anxiety.

In a systematic meta-analysis of psychological treatments for irritable bowel syndrome, Axelsson et al. (2023) searched 11 databases for relevant studies and found 118 reports published between 1983 and 2022. After a methodological quality selection, they used data from 62 studies (6,496 participants) and found that exposure therapy and hypnotherapy both had a positive impact when compared with control conditions. When their analysis included potential confounding variables, they found that exposure therapy had a greater impact than hypnotherapy. The authors concluded that exposure therapy appeared to be a promising treatment for irritable bowel syndrome.

Emotional exposure in schema coaching

When coaching clients want to deal with early maladaptive schema it can be very beneficial to encourage then to engage in recurring interaction with their fears or discomforts (McCormick, 2022). Clients can learn to cope with their unpleasant emotions more easily by facing their feared or frustrating situations repeatedly and realising that the outcomes of these are harmless and the consequences are minor (Roediger et al., 2018).

Some examples of emotional exposure exercises for the most frequent challenges in schema coaching are shown below.

For concerns about lack of support from others, the client purposely does important but not urgent work tasks, does not seek help, and endures the discomfort caused by the lack of support.

Five possible specific emotional exposure actions for the lack of support schema are:

1   Talking to team members that have co-operated well on a successful project about the support they have had from each other and tolerating any bad feelings that arise when discussing this.
2   Reviewing your career and thinking about what additional support you could have had from others and accepting any discomfort.
3   Thinking about an upcoming area of work and the level of support that you would ideally want, then comparing this to the level you are likely to get and enduring the bad feeling.
4   Going to a work prize giving or staff recognition event, talking to the winner about the level of support they got to do their job and tolerating the disquiet.
5   Calculating your net worth and considering how much more you may have had if you had obtained the ideal level of financial support and accepting any uneasiness.

For anxiety about excessive involvement with others, the person acts independently to purposely develop their own sense of identity and discover that other's disapproval is either absent or mild.

Six possible specific emotional exposure actions are:

1   Build your sense of preference by eating lunch at different cafés each day for a week and deciding which you like best while tolerating the indecision.
2   Reading the news on totally different web sites from your usual ones just to decide what you like best and why.
3   Emailing an acquaintance about having a coffee just to expand your social network and your sense of identity.
4   Meeting up with a trusted friend and sharing something personal with them to expand your emotional vulnerability and development.
5   Working to find one new possible friend this year.
6   Disagreeing with your partner about a trivial matter, just to exercise your sense of identity.

For failure fears, the individual asks for feedback, experiences any resulting feelings of 'failure', critically questions their schema inducing thoughts and tolerates the uncomfortable feelings.

Six possible specific emotional exposure actions are:

1   Buying a lottery ticket, and if you lose, engaging your healthy adult mode to reassure yourself that this is not a personal failure.
2   Writing a list of your achievements and telling yourself that despite the frequent feeling of being a failure, you have achieved a great deal.
3   Doing something that is a little outside your comfort zone, such as talking to a stranger and watching to see if they reject you or not, tolerating any discomfort.
4   Comparing yourself with a peer who has not done as well as you and so challenging your sense of inadequacy.
5   Deliberately doing something that you know you will fail at, such as running nonstop for an hour, feeling the sense of failure and realising it is unpleasant but not catastrophic.
6   Asking a friend for some direct honest feedback in an area where you know you do not do well and accepting any bad feelings.

When feeling overly controlled, the person requests ideas on how a task can be better done, frankly evaluates the options and chooses which ideas are helpful and more importantly which will be disregarded.

Six possible specific emotional exposure actions are:

1   Deliberately expressing an alternative perspective in a staff meeting.
2   Stating directly to a friend your preference for a movie to watch.
3   Asking for a main dish in a restaurant that you know your partner would not approve of.
4   Asking a peer for feedback on a project and deliberately only adopting some of the suggestions and ignoring others.
5   Deliberately disagreeing with your partner about an issue, just to exercise your own sense of control.
6   Discussing with a friend or partner what you want to do for your next holiday, independent of whether they will agree with you or not.

When needing excessive approval, the client purposely undertakes minor tasks that others may not approve of, but which the client thinks are useful. In this way the client confronts their deeply held need for approval by others.

Six possible specific emotional exposure actions are:

1   Complaining about the poor service at a restaurant or retail store.
2   Taking an item back to a store and saying you want your money back.
3   Doing something minor that you know annoys your partner.

4   Disagreeing over the timing of a project with your boss and tolerating any bad feelings.
5   Taking an alternative perspective in a discussion with friends and accepting any resulting feelings.
6   Participating in a street protest when you know that there will be onlookers who disagree with you.

Confronting persistent pessimism – when the client encounters negative or less than ideal situations, they can become aware of their negative thinking and consciously start to recognise the positive aspects or opportunities.

Six possible specific emotional exposure actions are:

1   Consider one bad news story in the media and look for a possible positive spin on it, for example a robbery that might result in the offenders being apprehended and the victims being given their goods back.
2   Deliberately being positive with friends when you first meet in the morning.
3   Starting a staff meeting by congratulating someone on a job they have done well.
4   Writing up a list of your achievements at the end of every month.
5   Asking a trusted friend what they see your strengths as.
6   Quietly watching others when walking down the street and imagining the range of good things these people have done in their lives.

When feeling a lack of spontaneity, the client can repeatedly explore new approaches or activities to build their opportunity for choice.

Six possible specific emotional exposure actions are:

1   Reading different magazines just to expand your options.
2   Driving a different way to work just for the fun of it.
3   Starting conversations with new team members at work just to see how it goes.
4   When buying a new piece of clothing, deliberately look at a wide range of options rather than just picking the brand you normally buy.
5   Undertaking random spontaneous acts of kindness for strangers.
6   Going on a holiday and only booking accommodation for the first few nights, being spontaneous about what you do next and tolerating the bad feelings.

For unrealistic striving, the client can intentionally undertake work tasks in a way that is not quite up to their typical exacting standards.

Six possible specific emotional exposure actions for unrealistic striving are:

1   Going home from work on time and striving to minimise the inner critic.
2   Writing an unimportant email and deliberately making one tiny error and tolerating the bad feelings.

3   Leaving work early and deliberately doing nothing, e.g., sitting in a chair in the sun and feeling how unpleasant but not disastrous it is.
4   Praising a team member in a one-on-one meeting and deliberately ignoring their mediocre performance in one or two areas.
5   Completing an important piece of work to a satisfactory but not immaculate level.
6   Making a few self-critical comments about your work in front of your team members.

Using these types of approaches clients can gradually learn to face their exaggerated concerns and find a more balanced and rational approach.

Case study: using emotional exposure in schema coaching

Jessica was the finance manager for a small professional service firm. She described herself as an introvert who did not like public speaking. Since her promotion from finance executive to finance manager she was expected to make a monthly presentation to the board of partners of the firm. She dreaded this and came to executive coaching to do something about it.

During the case conceptualisation it became clear that Jessica came from a family of shy individuals and so never had a good role model for public speaking. Her father was a tax accountant and her mother a financial auditor so doing accounting at university just seemed natural to Jessica. She had done well both at school and at university and went on to find a job with a large accounting firm shortly after graduation. She had stayed with the large firm for seven years but in the end felt that she was being overlooked for promotion because of her quiet manner. She then moved to the small professional services firm as a finance executive and enjoyed the family-like culture of the firm.

Jessica's coaching goal was to be able to give monthly presentations to the board of partners without undue stress or anxiety. The coach started with a solution-focused coaching approach and asked her how she would behave if she was not at all anxious giving presentations. Jessica said she would find it easy to prepare for the presentation because she would not be anticipating the anxiety associated with the board meetings. She would then wait calmly for the chair of the meeting to work through the minutes of the last meeting and the CEO's report before asking Jessica to present the financials. When she got up to speak, she would do so in a loud and confident manner and not just present the numbers but more importantly discuss her insights on the revenue and profitability trends.

When asked if some board presentations were better than others, Jessica said that they were all bad. So, the coach asked what she did to try and calm her nerves before a board meeting and Jessica said that very little helped. The coach felt a bit stuck at this point so decided to try a different approach.

When asked what she did to relax after work Jessica said she listened to classical music and walked. The coach asked if she had ever done yoga or meditation, or any other form of relaxation and Jessica said she had tried meditation, but it had not worked well for her and in fact seemed to make her more anxious. The coach then introduced the idea of progressive deep muscle relaxation as an approach to learning to relax and Jessica said that she was happy to try this.

In the next session the coach explained that deep muscle relaxation was a type of exercise that can significantly reduce stress and anxiety in the body by slowly and systematically releasing tension in different muscle groups in the body. He explained that the exercise can provide clients with an immediate sense of relaxation and Jessica said she was willing to try this.

The coach asked Jessica to sit back in the chair and get comfortable, to shut her eyes and take a few very slow breaths, filling her lungs, holding her breath and slowly releasing the breath and letting the tension in her body go. Jessica was then asked to focus on her feet, to tense them by curling up her toes and arching her foot, holding this tension, noticing what the tension felt like and then releasing it.

Following this, Jessica and the coach worked on tensing and relaxing muscle groups in the calves, thighs, hips, stomach, chest, back, arms and finally the head. The coach then asked Jessica to check back over her body and to release any residual tension that she could feel. Finally, she was asked to take a deep breath and then relax, saying silently to herself, 'calm and relaxed, calm and relaxed'.

At the end of the exercise Jessica said that she felt so much more relaxed and agreed with the coach that she would practice the deep muscle relaxation every day for the next two weeks. The coach said he would email her a sound file of the relaxation that she could listen to when practising.

In the next session Jessica reported that she had greatly enjoyed the relaxation and found it very useful, but that she was still anxious about giving board presentations. The coach suggested that they draw up a fear ladder or hierarchy of public speaking situations from minimally anxiety provoking to very frightening. The list from low to high was:

1 Talking to friends during a morning coffee.
2 Discussing a finance issue one on one with the CEO.
3 Going over a financial report with the CEO.
4 Being asked simple questions about the financial position of the firm by partners in her office.
5 Being asked complex questions about the financial position of the firm by partners in her office.
6 Having a meeting with a small group of friendly partners to discuss a financial issue.

7 Having a meeting with a small group of argumentative partners about a financial issue.
8 Discussing complex partner remuneration issues with the CEO and chair of the board.
9 Making a presentation to the full board on the financial position of the firm.
10 Being challenged and asked complex accounting questions by a group of argumentative partners in a full board meeting.

Over the next four sessions the coach went through the deep muscle relaxation exercise and worked slowly up the fear ladder until Jessica could imagine delivering a presentation to the board without undue anxiety.

After this Jessica began to deliberately set up meetings with the CEO and the chair of the board to discuss financial issues. Before each of these meetings she would book a private meeting room, practice her relaxation and mentally rehearse the discussion while in a calm state.

This process worked very well for three months but then Jessica reported that she had a setback. She had been confidently presenting to the board when an older cantankerous partner had started arguing with her about remuneration levels. She said that she suddenly felt weak at the knees and had to sit down. She felt that it was very unfair for this partner to speak to her in this way and that she could not find a convincing counter argument. Fortunately, the chair of the board had intervened at this point and said that the remuneration would be discussed later in the meeting. This had calmed Jessica's nerves, so that she was then able to continue on with her presentation in a satisfactory way.

The coach explained that the purpose of the graduated exposure training was not to eliminate all anxiety from every situation but was designed to enable Jessica to handle most situations without *undue* anxiety. 'Everyone feels anxious when they are ambushed like that in public, I certainly would!' said the coach. They went on to discuss how Jessica could thank the chair of the board for her intervention in the meeting and get her agreement that if similar situations were to arise in the future, she would do the same.

At the end of the session Jessica said that she felt a lot better about this ambush and now understood that her high expectations of almost never feeling anxious again, were unhelpful.

At the three month follow up Jessica said that she had been able to continue to practice the deep muscle relaxation when she needed and although she did not enjoy giving board presentations, she was able to do so in a reasonably relaxed manner. She said that the exposure training had been very helpful in providing her with a safe and systematic way of facing her fears.

Reflective practice exercise: Emotional exposure

Think of and write down below an irrational fear or dislike of something minor that you have in your life.

> Example: When not undertaking face to face coaching, I work in an open plan office and really dislike the noise around me, particularly the loud voice of the guy who sits opposite me.

Review the emotional exposure idea in this chapter and develop a list of things that you can intentionally do to counter your fear or dislike.

> Example: I could get a pair of noise cancelling headphones, listen to calming music and so block out the noise. However, I do not want to permanently do this. Over time I want to build my tolerance for the noise.

To ensure that you follow through with your emotional exposure who can you talk to about what you are going to do and why? Ask them to hold you accountable.

> Example: I can talk to my wife about the situation and agree that each day for two weeks I will wear the headphones but over time I will turn the music down and then turn off the noise cancelling so I gradually get used to the noise. She will be interested in this and so hold me accountable.

Review how you got on undertaking this exposure exercise and decide what you learned about yourself and the frustrations or anxieties that you have.

> Example: I have been using this approach for two weeks now and really see that when I have a degree of control over the noise, I can gradually expose myself to it and build up my tolerance.

Can you apply emotional exposure in your coaching practice and how would you do this?

> Example: When I first read about emotional exposure, I felt it was only relevant to phobias, but now I see that I can help my clients to build tolerance and resilience in all sorts of areas by using it.

Key learning points

- Exposure therapy is an evidence-based approach that assists clients to confront their fears or other situations that they routinely avoid.

- Therapeutic exposure can involve imagined, in vivo or virtual exposure. It can also involve interoceptive exposure or having the client generate feared physical sensations and learning that these are harmless.
- Exposure can be undertaken gradually or rapidly, with or without relaxation training.
- There has been a great deal of research demonstrating the effectiveness of exposure therapy.
- Exposure techniques can usefully be adapted to schema coaching for clients in the workplace.

Discussion topics

Discuss your current case load and decide if you have any clients who could benefit from emotional exposure.

What types of emotional exposure are best suited to the coaching population, imagined exposure, in vivo, virtual or interoceptive exposure? Why?

What speeds of exposure would suit your coaching population, rapid flooding, gradual *in vivo* exposure or systematic desensitisation.

Suggested reading

Foa, E., Hembree, E. A., Rothbaum, B. O. & Rauch, S. (2019). *Prolonged Exposure Therapy for PTSD: Emotional Processing of Traumatic Experiences − Therapist Guide*. Oxford University Press.

McMahon, G. (2011). *No More Stress! Be your Own Stress Management Coach*. Routledge.

Williams, C. (2012). *Overcoming Anxiety, Stress and Panic: A Five Areas Approach*. Routledge.

Chapter 14

Schema homework

This chapter introduces the importance of clients working on schema change processes between coaching sessions no matter which therapeutic approach the coach has used. This is essential as coaching involves action-based discussions with clients and follow up, not just inactive analytic conversations. This chapter outlines the recommendations for ensuring that homework is effective no matter whether foundation or more advanced techniques are being used. These recommendations include that homework needs to be clear with specific actions, timeframes and personal accountability, the rationale for the homework must be explained and understood and it must be discussed with the client and modified if the client has concerns. It should be reviewed in subsequent sessions in a supportive and empathetic manner so that lessons can be learned, and all progress made can be recognised. The chapter includes a review of the research into the effectiveness of therapeutic homework, an illustrative case study, a reflective practice exercise, key learning points, discussion topics and suggested further reading.

Introduction

Successful coaches need to ensure that they are involved in action-based discussions with clients and not just inactive analytic conversations (Pugh & Broome, 2020). Schema coaching homework involves the client undertaking schema change actions between coaching sessions so that they reduce the negative impact of their schema, strengthen their healthy adult and better manage dysfunctional thoughts, feelings and behaviour (McCormick, 2022). This active highly experiential focus helps clients to better deal with long standing challenges that they have not been able to change using other less active approaches.

Homework or therapeutic actions undertaken between sessions are critical to nearly all psychotherapy and particularly to cognitive behavioural therapy (Haller & Watzke, 2021). Homework involves carrying out actions between sessions to ensure that the client builds skills (Kazantzis & L'Abate 2007, Lambert et al., 2007). It exists in many forms of psychotherapy and is an

DOI: 10.4324/9781003501824-14

evidence-based approach that assists clients to practice adaptive behaviours so that they are more likely to generalise to real world situations. For example in the case of the schema challenge card outlined in Chapter 8, the client learns to use the technique in the session but then outside the coaching office they write down any triggering event, the subsequent emotion, the likely connection between the situation, the schema and the emotion, the dysfunctional thinking that reinforces this link, their challenge to these unhelpful thoughts, their coping actions undertaken and finally the lessons they learn. Repeated practice not only enhances but also maintains functional change (Kazantzis & Ronan, 2006).

Coaching homework has the following benefits no matter which therapeutic techniques are used:

- It provides much greater opportunity for practice than available during the coaching session.
- It helps the client to build skills and capability.
- It can help to develop greater self confidence in clients.
- It will help the coach to gain insights into what works and does not work for the client.
- It enables the coach to review progress in a way that cannot easily be done inside a session.

The success or otherwise of the implementation needs to be discussed at subsequent coaching sessions. This helps lessons to be learned and refinements to the homework made.

The effectiveness of homework

For homework to be effective, Beck et al. (1979) suggests the following:

1   The homework needs to be clear with specific actions, timeframes and personal accountability.
2   The rationale for the homework must be explained and understood by the client.
3   The client's response to the suggested homework needs to be carefully listened to and changes made if the client has concerns.
4   Homework implementation needs to be reviewed in subsequent sessions in a supportive and empathetic manner so that lessons can be learned and all progress made can be recognised.

Research into homework has primarily been undertaken in the therapeutic area. However, given the overlap between coaching and therapy this research can provide any coach with some confidence that they are using evidence-based tools.

In an early study Broder (2000) argued for the use of homework to enhance the therapeutic effectiveness of rational emotive/cognitive behavioural therapy. The author suggested that useful homework techniques included readings, goal setting, scaling, mood management, thought disputation, repeating affirmations, mood diary keeping, list making, guided imagery, structured visualisation, relaxation and meditation, exposure, and thought stopping.

In a replication and extension of an earlier meta-analysis on homework effects in cognitive and behavioural therapy Kazantzis et al. (2010) reviewed 46 studies with 1,072 subjects and found that homework had a strong positive impact on pre–posttreatment assessment. The authors concluded that there was support for homework assignments enhancing therapy outcomes with depressed clients.

In an updated meta-analysis of research undertaken since 2000, Mausbach et al. (2010) reviewed the impact of homework compliance on treatment outcomes. They reviewed 23 studies with 2,183 clients and their results indicated a significant relationship between homework and therapy outcome with a small to medium effect size. Their work indicated that these results were robust across target symptoms (e.g., for both depression or anxiety), the source of the homework rating (e.g., both client and therapist ratings), the timing of the homework rating (e.g., after the fact or during the therapy) and type of homework measure (e.g., rating scales of level of homework completed).

Kazantzis et al. (2016) argued that homework assignments produced both causal and correlational benefits but that previous research had focused on the amount of compliance (i.e., quantity), and not on skill acquisition (i.e., quality). The authors therefore undertook a meta-analysis of homework adherence, quantity and quality. They used 17 studies of cognitive behaviour therapy that focused on a positive impact at posttreatment and follow up. This study suggested that homework quantity and quality were both useful measures of homework impact on therapy outcome.

Homework is a useful approach for decreasing the level of depression symptoms in clients when telephone-based cognitive behaviour therapy was used (Haller & Watzke, 2021). However, the authors noted that more research was needed into how telephone-based cognitive behaviour therapy impacts the relationship between depression symptoms and homework.

Ryum et al. (2023) undertook a systematic review with 25 studies with 1,304 clients and 118 therapists, that used cognitive behavioural therapy with depression and anxiety disorders. They found that therapists that presented a sound rationale for the homework, collaboratively designed it, planned and reviewed the homework tasks in line with the clients' goals, aligned the homework with the important insights from the session and used a written summary of the homework and its rationale improved its impact.

Marchena Giráldez et al. (2023) aimed to determine how behavioural therapists assign therapeutic tasks and reviewed their compliance. They used observational methods to analyse the verbal interaction in 211 recorded sessions. They found that successful behavioural psychologists used motivating comments when giving homework. At follow up successful therapists frequently gave positive reinforcement when clients completed their homework, but they stopped the review process when homework was only partly or not completed.

The above review suggests that therapists and coaches can have some confidence in the value of using between session homework to enhance client outcomes.

Schema coaching homework

Schema coaching, when applied effectively, relies on the client's active participation in actions that challenge their dysfunctional schemas and reinforce their healthy adult mindset (Roediger et al., 2018). Like psychotherapy, schema coaching homework involves tasks that clients undertake between coaching sessions. These assignments serve two purposes: addressing underlying needs and enhancing the management of dysfunctional thoughts, feelings, and behaviours (McCormick, 2022).

To facilitate the homework process, Roediger et al. (2018) recommends creating a log for clients that enables them to record their completed tasks and the outcomes. The format can be simple, such as a paper or phone-based document, a spreadsheet, or a cloud-based shared file accessible to both parties.

When clients are unwilling or unable to complete their homework, this information becomes crucial for discussion in subsequent coaching sessions. Reasons for non-completion could vary: the task might not resonate with the client, they may have faced illness, hardship, a crisis, or perhaps the assignment felt too challenging or intimidating. These insights provide valuable lessons for how the coach can progress and adapt. Understanding client engagement and barriers to homework completion is essential for effective coaching and positive outcomes.

To help clients develop sound schema homework habits they can be encouraged to:

- Set specific time aside to undertake it with suitable smartphone calendar reminders.
- Start with smaller and easier to achieve tasks and progress to more demanding ones.
- Record progress honestly making it clear what worked and what did not.
- Repeatedly practicing new thinking patterns or helpful behaviours.

There are many different types of useful schema coaching exercises that can be used as homework (Roediger et al., 2018). For example, a log sheet can be used to record:

1   Triggering events for schema and modes.
2   Resulting thoughts, feelings, emotions, moods, images, bodily sensations.
3   Inner critic and healthy adult voices.
4   Coping mechanisms and actions.
5   Conversations with important others about troubling events or memories and what has been done to deal with these.
6   Lessons learned from events and important incidents.

Schema homework exercises can be used to address issues in three areas – cognitive, perception-focused and physical activities (Roediger et al., 2018). All these exercises are designed to decrease the amount of time the client spends in unhelpful rumination, to bring the client's attention back to the present moment and to develop effective coping behaviours.

The range of cognitive-focused homework activities adapted from Roediger et al. (2018) include:

- Body scan meditations which are a specific type of mindfulness meditation that helps clients to systematically focus their attention on their bodies. During a body scan, clients systematically direct their awareness to different parts of their body, observing tensions, sensations, and any other physical experiences. The aim of body scan meditations is typically to build awareness of the sensations, as well as their ebb and flow, rather than to change or relax away tensions. The client is invited to note when their mind wanders and then to gently guide it back to the practice.
- Expressive writing – which helps the client to express emotions about individuals who have caused trauma injury or pain to them in the past. This is best done in a spontaneous manner with a client writing down whatever comes to mind. There is little value in the client spending time editing or rewriting such expressive prose.
- Inspirational readings – these are quotes, stories, poems, books, prayers or meditations that are designed to provide valuable life lessons, to improve motivation and to uplift the client's mood. They can be asked to undertake an internet search on inspirational readings that are relative to their challenges, to record these and read these back to the coach in the subsequent session. The choices made by the client can provide valuable insights for the coach into the manner and style of motivation that is helpful to reinforce change.
- Counting numbers can be helpful to disrupt ruminations, with exercises such as counting down from 100 by 8s and other variations.
- Guided imagery techniques: these involve the client creating vivid mental pictures to induce specific experiences, feelings or sensations. The process may start with the coach guiding the client in a brief relaxation process. The coach then assists the client to create a mental image of a specific scene or scenario and asks questions to help make these images as

realistic as possible. The technique can help the client to practice new helpful behaviours or reshape unproductive thoughts and actions.

- Letter writing – this approach involves writing never-to-be-sent letters to the individuals in the client's life who have been vindictive or unhelpful. This is very often a cathartic experience for the client that helps them to let go of archaic pain. It can also be useful for the client to write to the parent or significant other as they were when the client was a child. This can be very helpful, for example, as some clients feel very angry at a parent because of the way they treated them as a child but actually now they like the parent all these years later because they have mellowed and are no longer cruel. This allows the client to write to the parent as they were years ago without feeling they are being disloyal to the parent as they are today.

- Ideal life exercise – in this exercise the client is asked to think about what sort of life they would like to live in say five, ten or 20 years. They are asked what sort of career they want, where would they like to live, what sort of leader they would like to be, what types of team members they would want and so on. This helps to move the client into positive future thinking and is a great start to any coaching programme.

- Light ball meditation – this is a form of meditation that involves the client sitting comfortably and then imagining the warm glow from a ball of light that surrounds their feet. The client then imagines the ball of light moving up their body and the warm glow permeating their legs, the torso, arms and finally their head. The visualisation helps the client to relax their body and steady their thoughts. When the client gets distracted, they simply bring their attention back to the light ball.

- Self-instructional training which is used to help clients challenge and change unhelpful beliefs and thoughts. In the coaching session, the client and coach work collaboratively to identify unhelpful thoughts such as 'I am a failure and will be found out at any moment'. If needed, the coach could model an appropriate dialogue and self-statements 'I am thinking that I am a failure, but I do know that this is not true.' The client then tries their own version of the self-instruction. The client and coach agree on where and when the client will practice this exercise. This process can reduce anxiety, assist with cognitive skill building and enhance the healthy adult mode.

- Watching thoughts – this is a form of meditation that helps the clients to observe their thoughts coming and then going from their consciousness. A useful analogy is for the client to see their thoughts as clouds in the sky or cars on a motorway – coming and going. With practice this meditation can help clients let go of unhelpful and intrusive ruminations.

A range of perception-focused techniques adapted from Roediger et al. (2018) include:

- Five senses meditation: this involves asking the client to relax and notice five things in the room that they can see, four things they can feel in their body, three things they can hear, two things they can smell and one thing they can taste. This is a very helpful way to enable the client to return to the present moment when they are caught up in problematic situations such as a difficult meeting.
- Focused attention: in this exercise the client is asked to take a slow deep breath and then to start to describe all the things they can see in detail. The client may describe the carpet, the furniture, the window frames, the view out the windows and the ceiling. This exercise also helps the client to return to the present moment and get clear of unhelpful or difficult perceptions.
- Observing self – this involves asking the client to see themselves and what they are doing from the perspective of a video camera. The client may see themselves sitting in a chair, inside a building, in the south side of the city, by the sea. The observing self is not a thought or a feeling but is an awareness of oneself and the surroundings. The observing self is that part of yourself that experiences, sees and touches but that does not change. Using this perspective helps the client to be non-judgemental and become more aware of what is going on. The client can learn that when they are having difficult thoughts they can step back and just observe – thus gaining some distance from them.
- Intensive listening: this teaches the client to connect with their surroundings. They are asked to name sounds, to identify their source, to discover how their mind and body reacts to the sounds and so on. The exercise builds awareness, acceptance and non-judgemental observation.
- Listening to music: for clients who are experiencing intense and unhelpful emotions such as anxiety, it can be very helpful for them to listen to loud music. This is best done with headphones and with music that creates positive and joyful emotions. The distraction and re-focusing can be very helpful.
- Mindful eating: involves asking the client to eat and to focus all their attention on the smell of the food, its texture, what it feels like in their mouth, the taste of the various elements of the food, the feeling of swallowing it, the aftertaste and so on. This exercise builds awareness and a present moment focus.

A range of physical activities adapted from Roediger et al. (2018) include:

- Activity logs: asking clients to keep records of physical activities between sessions can be extremely helpful in providing the coach with real world data. It can also be helpful for the client to build awareness and to gain insight into the relationship between physical activities and their emotions. One simple example is to ask the client to keep a log of their physical exercise levels and mood. This may just be three columns, the date, the number of minutes of physical exercise and a 'smiley face' to record happy, neutral or sad.

- Diaphragmatic breathing: a helpful homework exercise for almost any client that reports feeling stress is to undertake breath work. Exercises may include diaphragmatic breathing where the client lies on their back, puts one hand on their upper chest and the other hand below their rib cage and slowly inhales and ensures that they can feel the breath moving all the way to their lower lungs. The sensation can be felt with the hand on the lower rib cage. This type of slow diaphragmatic breathing can enable the client to feel more relaxed and in control.
- Intensive exercise: encouraging the client to undertake supervised intensive physical exercise can be very helpful to build fitness and lift depressive moods.
- Mindful physical activities: the client is encouraged to pay close attention to regular activities and to remain in the moment. This might include building mindful awareness when walking, cleaning teeth, doing dishes and so on. Present moment mindfulness often helps clients to reduce the amount of future-focused worry time or past-focused thinking about regrets.
- Self-care physical activities: many clients are highly self-critical and helping them to care for themselves better can be very beneficial. Self-care activities may include yoga, tai chi, better hydration, relaxing baths, massage and so on.
- Square breathing: this is an exercise to slow down breathing. The client is asked to slowly exhale, then slowly inhale to the count of four, to hold the breath for four, to exhale for four and hold for four. This exercise can be very useful in reducing stress and anxiety.

In addition to the above homework exercises, most of the chapters in this book describe techniques that can be turned into activities to be undertaken between sessions. Examples are mindful release in Chapter 7, schema challenge in Chapter 8, imagery rescripting in Chapter 11, chairwork and dialogue techniques in Chapter 12 and emotional exposure exercises in Chapter 13.

Case study: schema homework

Aleena was the People and Culture Manager for a government department. She reported to the General Manager Corporate Services. She had five people in her team who were focused on recruitment, employment relations, people management issues, change processes and upskilling people leaders. Aleena had seven years of HR experience, including forming high trust relationships, building workplace culture, performance management and leadership development. She worked very long hours and was typically tired and exhausted by the end of the week. She often spent much of the weekend sleeping and this was having a serious impact on the relationship with her partner.

Aleena came to coaching wanting to find better work life balance and to improve her relationship with the General Manager Corporate Services. She also felt her team was a group of siloed specialists rather than a fully functioning integrated team and wanted to change this.

When asked what she wanted to start the coaching with, Aleena said it was improving her work life balance. As a homework exercise at the end of the first session the coach asked Aleena to write about what her ideal life would look like. Aleena was not sure where to start so the coach suggested the following instructions and prompt questions.

'Write about what your ideal life would look like in some detail. Give yourself time to think, imagine and dream before you start writing, if this helps. Visualise yourself in ten years' time and think about the following questions:

- What will you have accomplished in your career?
- What kinds of team would you have reporting to you?
- What sort of leader would you like to report to?
- What will you have accomplished in your personal life?
- What kinds of friends would you have?
- What would your ideal day look like?
- What would a great year be like?
- What sorts of holidays would you have?'

Aleena came back to the next coaching session apologising that she had very little time to undertake the ideal life exercise but that she had written a few bullet points.

These were – 'In ten years' time, ideally, I would:

- Be the People and Culture Manager for a larger organisation.
- I would have great people in my team who would all have a common goal and a unified purpose rather than be siloed specialists.
- I would have a positive supportive leader, unlike my current boss.
- I would be happy at home and have time to garden and walk the dog.
- I would have time to spend with my friends – at least once a fortnightly Friday lunch.
- My ideal day would be no more than ten hours.
- My year would include four weeks uninterrupted holiday'.

The coach asked Aleena what she had learned from undertaking the homework and she said bluntly 'I am in the wrong job, I have the wrong boss, I have the wrong team'. The coach asked Aleena what she wanted to do, and she said 'This homework exercise was just great. I have been working so hard that I have not had any time to think about what I want in life. However, now

I have started to think about this I know I need to find another job. This time I will be very careful to assess the calibre of the leader who I will work for. This really is the critical issue. I want a supportive boss, to be able to hire the right team, to build the right capabilities, to delegate and to find myself'.

Reflective practice exercise: designing homework

Write down an area of your life you would like to change. Pick an area that is simple and clear rather than complex and existential.

Example: I would like to worry less before seeing clients for coaching.

Undertake the ideal life exercise and write about how you ideally want to live your life and be sure you include what you want in the area you wrote about above.

Example: In my ideal life I would have a thriving coaching practice and look forward to all my client sessions.

Read over the wide range of homework exercises outlined above and pick one example that you can use to make the change in your life that you want.

Example: I will use the square breathing and the imagery exercises.

Write your action plan below.

Example: Every day for the next week I will spend five minutes before my coaching sessions to do square breathing and imagining myself being calm and highly tuned into the client.

How will you hold yourself accountable to complete your homework?

Example: I will talk to my supervisor about my concerns and the homework exercises and then I will talk about the outcomes later on with her.

Key learning points

- Schema coaching homework involves the client undertaking schema change actions between coaching sessions so that they reduce the negative impact of schema, strengthen their healthy adult and better manage dysfunctional thoughts, feelings and behaviour.
- For homework to be effective, it needs to be clear with specific actions, timeframes and personal accountability. The rationale must be explained and understood by the client. Changes to the suggested homework should

be made if the client has concerns. Homework implementation needs to be reviewed in subsequent sessions so that lessons can be learned, and all progress made can be recognised.

- A review of the literature suggests that coaches can have some confidence in the value of using between session homework to enhance client outcomes
- Effective schema homework exercise exists in three areas: cognitive, perception-focused and physical activity homework.

Discussion topics

Discuss how often you agree homework with your coaching clients. What types of homework do you usually use? How effective is it?

Read over the range of suggested homework exercises in this chapter and identify ones that you want to use more in future. Why did you pick these exercises?

How will you evaluate the effectiveness of the homework that you use?

Suggested readings

Broder, M. S. (2000). Making optimal use of homework to enhance your therapeutic effectiveness. *Journal of rational-emotive and cognitive-behavior therapy*, 18(1), 3–18.

Jongsma Jr, A. E. & Bruce, T. J. (2021). *Adult psychotherapy homework planner*. John Wiley & Sons.

Kazantzis, N., Whittington, C., Zelencich, L., Kyrios, M., Norton, P. J. & Hofmann, S. G. (2016). Quantity and quality of homework compliance: A meta-analysis of relations with outcome in cognitive behavior therapy. *Behavior Therapy*, 47(5), 755–772. doi:10.1016/j.beth.2016.05.002.

Chapter 15

Integrating the approach

This chapter shows the coach how to bring together all the schema techniques set out in the book in an integrated way. In this circumstance, integrative means to co-ordinate or blend these approaches into an effective unified approach. In coaching integration is relevant because client difficulties often have several sources, so using a single therapeutic method may not be successful. Using the integrative approach the coach will typically use one coaching methodology during a session but add a small number of therapeutic techniques as is appropriate for the individual client. The rationale for the approach needs to be explained in simple clear terms to the client. This chapter sets out a case study on using the integrated approach, a reflective practice exercise, key learning points, discussion topics and suggested further reading.

What an integrative coaching approach is

According to the Merriam-Webster dictionary integrative means to form, co-ordinate or blend into a functioning or unified whole (Merriam-Webster, 2021). In coaching or therapy integration is important because client challenges often have multiple causes, so using just one single therapeutic method is not likely to be successful (Cooper & McLeod, 2007). Nothing is appropriate in all situations as different clients are helped by different processes at different times. McCormick (2023a) suggests that integrative coaching means that the coach will typically use one coaching approach or methodology during a session but add a small number of therapeutic techniques as is appropriate for the individual client. The rationale and nature of these techniques needs to be explained in simple clear terms to the client. If the coach is struggling to explain the rationale, then they should ask if their approach is appropriate. Research into the use of an integrative approach suggests that a range of therapeutic techniques can be usefully used, even when the underlying theories are not entirely congruent, provided their use can be explained in simple clear language (Castonguay & Beutler, 2006; Cooper, 2008).

DOI: 10.4324/9781003501824-15

For example, a coach may begin working with a client using the GROW (Goal, Reality, Options and Way forward) model but find that the client is unable to develop options for effectively dealing with their challenges. At this point the coach may introduce the ACT (Acceptance and Commitment Therapy) model and ask the client if accepting the reality of their challenges and letting go of the associated self-criticism, may be helpful. If the client is willing to try out this approach the coach may explain it in more detail, undertake one or two experiential exercises and agree ACT-based homework with the client. The homework setting element of the session is clearly an integration with the 'Way forward' step in the GROW model.

The integrative schema coaching approach

Schema coaching integrates a range of different techniques from cognitive behavioural, gestalt and psychodynamic therapy as well as attachment and object relations theories (McCormick, 2022). This integration is based on the collaborative schema assessment and case conceptualisation phase. The schema that the client and coach identify is then dealt with using the range of schema coaching techniques such as mindful release, schema challenge, imagery rescripting, chairwork or emotional exposure. The integration inherent in schema coaching is easily explained to client by making it clear that this approach will provide a toolkit of techniques all of which are useful in dealing with their unhelpful schema. The coach can also explain that schema coaching uses techniques that deal with different aspects of the presenting issue, for example, painful memories (imagery rescripting), unhelpful thinking (schema challenge), behavioural avoidance (emotional exposure) and so on.

Case study: the integrative schema coaching approach

Dina was an entrepreneur who had a background in operations research and had developed software packages for the optimisation of company resources and process flows. She had grown the company from a classic garage start up to a multi-million-dollar business with over 40 staff. She was energised, brash and running at a hundred miles an hour.

She came to executive coaching after the company had been approached by a large competitor in the business optimisation space who had said they wanted to make a full takeover offer. At first Dina had been absolutely delighted by the acquisition possibility but suddenly in subsequent meetings with the potential acquirer she had developed deeply troubling feelings verging on panic attacks. Dina felt that these had 'erupted out of nowhere'. She not only had no idea of their origin but also no experience or techniques to deal with them. She described the attacks as terrifying and as if she was going to have a heart attack and a brain haemorrhage, all at once.

In the initial session, the coach suggested that Dina see her doctor and have a thorough medical check-up. She subsequently reported back that the doctor had given her the all clear, that her blood pressure and blood tests were in the normal range, as was her heart function. The doctor had said that she felt that the panic attacks had a psychological origin but would likely decrease over time.

At Dina's request, they spent the next session exploring the build-up to the acquisition offer and the nature of the first two meetings with the acquirer. Dina said that in the first meeting she was so shocked and delighted that she did not register much. However, in the second meeting, she had been deeply impacted by the CEO of the acquirer. He was a big muscular man with slicked back hair and a gruff manner. Dina said that he reminded her of her stepfather who had died a decade ago. She said that ever since meeting him she had started to feel uncomfortable and to wonder if the potential acquisition would go ahead. She felt quite a bit of pressure from the angel investors who had put money into the company at its outset and who now were very keen to sell their shares and realise a profit. Dina had started to feel as if she wanted to avoid any subsequent meetings with the CEO but knew that this was utterly impossible. She felt trapped and deeply anxious.

The coach spent the next session teaching Dina about the nature of the human stress response. He explained that stressful situations, no matter their cause often triggered a surge of stress hormones that in turn produced a well-defined set of physiological responses. Stressful situations often led to increases in heart rate, rapid breathing, tightened muscles and increased sweating. The coach explained that while long-term unrelenting stress was bad for physical and psychological health, short-term stresses were rarely dangerous. Dina said her panic attacked certainly did feel dangerous and the coach empathised but said despite the extremely bad feelings the doctors report suggested that no damage had been done to her.

The coach suggested that in the next session he teach Dina deep muscle relaxation and that they start a form of safe gradual emotional exposure training called systematic desensitization. Dina was in full agreement. Over the course of the next two sessions and with a considerable amount of determined homework, Dina made excellent progress. This initial training was enough to reduce Dina's stress response in the negotiation sessions and to remove her desire to avoid the meetings. While good progress was being made, Dina was determined to continue with the coaching and to 'get to the bottom of the issue'.

At this point the coach asked Dina if she felt that the memories of her stepfather were important in the development of her anxiety and she said 'Yes, that's a hidden weeping sore'. The coach then discussed the nature of schema coaching, and particularly the imagery rescripting technique. He said that imagery rescripting was an experiential approach that used imagery and imagination to intervene in difficult memories and to change the outcome and impact of the memory. Dina was fascinated and keen to try the approach in the next session.

In the imagery rescripting session Dina chose to work on a painful memory that happened when she was about 10 years old. She was doing her homework when her stepfather told her to make him a cup of tea. She did this but when she went to bring him the tea she tripped and spilled the hot liquid over his lap. He was furious and yelled that she was a 'stupid, good-for-nothing girl who would never amount to anything'. Dina was crushed by the outburst and went to find her mother. Unfortunately, her mother was at the supermarket at the time and Dina had to wait crying and deeply fearful of her stepfather and what he might do to her.

In the imagery rescripting session the coach asked Dina to close her eyes and tell the story in the first person present 'I am a ten-year-old girl, and I am doing my homework when my stepfather demands that I make him a cup of tea ...'. Just at the point of slipping and spilling the drink, the coach intervened in the story and said that while stepfather was hurt and angry, he was not to yell at her. Also, in this version the mother arrived home from the supermarket immediately after the accident and was able to comfort Dina. At the end of the imagery session, Dina said that she felt somehow the memory had less power and that she felt hugely comforted by her mother's care and affection.

In the next session, the coach introduced the idea of the schema challenge card and explained that Dina's thinking patterns were probably compounding the anxiety in the moments before the panic feelings set in. Dina and the coach worked on ways that she could alter her thinking and tell herself that while her anxiety was deeply unpleasant it would not lead to a heart attack or a brain haemorrhage.

At this point Dina said that she was feeling much better about the acquisition process and was better able to understand the nature of her stress response and to act in a way that minimised it. In particular she said it was very useful to have learned a range of techniques that were all able to help her deal with her anxiety. The coach said 'I am delighted that the integrated techniques of schema coaching are so helpful to you'.

Key learning points

- Integrative means to form, co-ordinate or blend into a functioning or unified whole.
- Integrative coaching means that the coach will use one approach during a session but add on a small number of therapeutic techniques as is appropriate for the individual client.
- The integration inherent in schema coaching can easily be described to the client by explaining that they will provide them with a toolkit of techniques all of which are useful in dealing with various aspects of the unhelpful schema.

Discussion topics

Why is schema coaching an integrated approach to dealing with client challenges? How does an integrated approach help the client?

Do you use a range of therapeutic techniques in your coaching? Which ones? Why do you use these?

If you use multiple therapeutic techniques in your coaching, do you explain the nature of the techniques to the client, ask permission to use them and show how they integrate with the coaching approach that you are using?

Selected readings

McCormick, I. A. (2023a). An introduction to schema coaching techniques, part 1: The schema octagon. *The Coaching Psychologist*, 19(1), 26–32.

McCormick, I. A. (2023b). Case conceptualisation using schema coaching analysis: an illustrative case study. *Coaching Psychology International*, 16(9), 1–7.

McCormick, I. A. (2023c). Chapter 11, An eclectic versus integrated approach to using therapeutic techniques in coaching. In *Reflective Practice for Coaches: A Guidebook for Advanced Professional Development*, pp. 151–156. Routledge.

McCormick, I. A. (2023d). Schema coaching techniques, part 2: Schema case conceptualisation and psychoeducation. *The Coaching Psychologist*, 19(2), 4–12.

Chapter 16

A client's guide to schema coaching

This guide provides a simple explanation of schema coaching which can be given to clients so that they can better understand what they are likely to see and experience before they start this type of coaching.

Some questions to start

- Do you find yourself repeatedly being drawn into patterns of unhelpful behaviour?
- Do you work extremely hard and have high standards but find it difficult to switch off, relax and just say – enough?
- Do you have a savage inner critic that seems to constantly put you down or stop you achieving more?

If any of these seem like you, then schema coaching could be for you.

Case study

Harry was a successful engineer who had led a construction support team for the last five years. Despite his success, he still reported being very nervous tendering for projects and in particular doing presentations in project bids. Harry described the problem as an overactive inner critic which was particularly troublesome in high demand situations.

The coach started by looking at what approaches Harry had already used to control his inner critic in the past and then looking at ways of strengthening these. However, after three sessions Harry said that he seemed to be quite unable to deal effectively with his inner critic and that the problem appeared to be deep-seated.

The coach then suggested that they look at schema coaching and Harry was keen to try this different approach, as he understood it was designed for people with more deep-seated problems. To understand the nature and development of the problem, the coach suggested that Harry spend some time during the session describing his parents, his upbringing and the formative stages of his inner critic. Harry described both his father and mother as being very critical of him

DOI: 10.4324/9781003501824-16

and that this attention was very intense as he was an only child. Harry had been a very meek boy who, despite an enduring sense of failure, had done reasonably well at school. However, at university he had spent time with a very influential lecturer who seemed to have taken a great liking to Harry. The lecturer explained that Harry was very talented, despite his nervousness and that he was very likely to have a promising career in engineering. The lecturer then helped Harry get his first job in a large professional service firm and Harry loved the work.

His early years in the firm had gone well but the inner critic started to become much louder as Harry became more senior and was expected to be part of a sales team for the firm.

Together Harry and the coach decided that the long-standing schema was a sense of failure and that at times of stress this was exacerbated by an overactive inner critic. Harry felt that understanding this was an important foundation to begin the schema coaching.

How schema coaching works

Schema coaching has two phases as set out below.

Assessment and education phase

This includes case conceptualisation where the client and coach work together to understand the client's challenges, how these issues started and what maintains them. Once a clear picture has been established, the coach helps the client to understand the nature of schemas (long-standing unhelpful patterns of thinking, feeling and behaviour) and modes (short-term mood states that are a response to schemas). For example, a client may learn about the subjugation schema and how allowing domination by their boss, wife and friends causes them to feel helpless and sad.

Change phase

In this phase the coach uses a range of different strategies to help the client alter the way they feel, think and behave.

The techniques include the following:

- Dialogue techniques which help clients to understand the different parts of themselves and the interaction between them, for example, the inner critic and healthy adult.
- Schema challenge that identifies the thinking process that helps to maintain the schema problem or distortion and provides the client with a systematic way to challenge and rethink the issue.
- Mindful release uses mindfulness techniques to help the client to let go of unhelpful memories, thoughts and feelings.

- Emotional exposure encourages the client to identify the ways in which they try to avoid schema-based pain. The technique involves providing a safe environment in which the client can gradually face what they are trying to avoid and so reduce the impact of it.
- Imagery rescripting, which is a powerful process that helps clients to identify and then change important early schema memories. It can redefine and create new neural networks and so reduce the intensity of the emotional connection to important memories.
- Relapse prevention involves the client and coach working to identify high-risk situations that may trigger unhelpful schema patterns and find ways to reduce the impact of these situations and so prevent relapse. It is a technique for maintaining progress after coaching has finished.

Schema – What They Are

Schema are enduring, typically negative, patterns that start in childhood or adolescence and have an impact throughout the person's life. We all view life through our schema lens. Schemas develop because the needs of the child are not met. These needs are for autonomy, competence and identity, the freedom to express healthy needs and emotions, secure attachment to caregivers and the ability to be spontaneous and play but to have reasonable limits and self-control. Schema are self-perpetuating, and people often structure their lives to prove they are true.

The schema frequently seen in coaching

After using the schema approach for many years with executives and team members in the workplace, the following maladaptive schema have been found to be most prevalent in this group:

1 Unrelenting striving: this is the most common seen in the competitive corporate or professional service environment. In this the client is extremely hard working and frequently believes that they must continue at this gruelling pace to meet their own and the organisations very high performance standards.
2 Sense of failure: this schema is commonly seen in leaders who have done very well or been promoted rapidly and at a pace they did not expect. They believe that despite their achievements in life, that they have failed, will fail, or that they are not as good or worthy as their peers.
3 Needing approval: this is commonly seen in executives with a sense of inadequacy or personal shortcoming and who despite their achievements, have a strong belief that they need too much attention approval or recognition from their manager, peers or team members.

4 Self-sacrifice: this is frequently seen in the health and other caring professions where clients are constantly exposed to individuals with very high and urgent needs. These people often feel that their own needs are unimportant and certainly can be almost endlessly delayed because of the intense and critical needs of others.

5 Lack of support: this is often seen in competitive organisations where corrosive politics are evident. The client has the belief that despite what they have already achieved in life that significant others have not supported them enough, financially, emotionally or career wise.

6 Excessive involvement with others: this is seen in clients who have an overly strong connection with a significant other such as a parent, teacher, leader or spouse. This connection means that the individual has little room to develop their own sense of self and is unsure of their own wants, desires, needs and value.

7 Pessimism: this is seen with clients who feel that they dwell too much on the betrayal, disappointments, losses, conflicts and failures of the past. They tend to minimise or trivialise the positive aspects of life.

8 Lack of spontaneity: this is seen in workers who feel that they must control, contain and suppress their natural spontaneous actions, communications or feelings because others may not approve or because they may not be able to control their expression once it starts.

9 Feeling controlled: this schema is seen in individuals who, despite having achieved a lot in their life and career, still often give up control of important areas to others. They will often hand over control of significant aspects in their own lives because the dominant figure is 'always right' or 'must be obeyed'.

In addition, there are a range of positive schema, which are set out below:

1 Emotional fulfilment and stable attachment: the belief that the person has someone who will listen and understand, nurture and care deeply about them.

2 Empathic consideration: the person feels that they can accept that they do not always have to get their own way in group decisions and can see others' perspectives.

3 Emotional openness: the person can show their emotions comfortably and feel that important others care about them, are expressive and spontaneous.

4 Developed self: the individual can establish an independent life and is not overly involved with their parents or care givers and their difficulties. They believe that their parents or care givers are not trying to live vicariously through them.

5 Healthy self-control: the person can discipline themselves enough to complete boring tasks and not easily give up.

6   Success: the person believes that they are as talented as most other people and usually do as well or better than others.
7   Optimism: the person generally feels safe and secure and believes that serious financial problems, illnesses, or catastrophic events are unlikely to happen to them.
8   Self-compassion and realistic expectations: the person believes that when they make a mistake, they can generally give themselves the benefit of the doubt, forgive themselves and they do not feel that they deserve punishment.
9   Social belonging: the person usually fits in and feels included in the groups they belong to.

Schema modes

Schema modes or moods are the present moment emotional phases and coping responses both positive and negative that we experience every day. Schema modes are typically caused by the things that happen to us – our emotional triggers.

In the context of a schema coaching session, we may see that a client with the needing approval schema may be ingratiating and warm at the beginning of the session but suddenly express the anger and resentment at not being able to be recognised by others.

Common types of schema modes include the following:

- Healthy adult mode in which the clients mature executive functioning is operating. They may be obtaining information, evaluating it or problem-solving in a balanced and rational way. In the healthy adult mode the client will take responsibility for their own actions, keep commitments and demonstrate emotional intelligence.
- Child mode in which the client expresses primitive and often repressed emotions when their needs are not met. The coach may suddenly see the following modes: the vulnerable child, the abandoned child, the abused child, the deprived child, or the rejected child.
- Inner critic modes in which the client's internalised core harmful messages, beliefs and judgements play loudly in their head. These can be punitive – 'You know that you are an idiot' or demeaning modes – 'You will fail at this one, for sure'.
- Maladaptive coping modes in which the client tries to deal with their unhelpful child and inner critic modes in a way that often makes the situation worse. Examples can include compliant surrender (giving in to the schema), detached protector (shutting down or zoning out), detached self-soother (anesthetising using drugs, self-stimulating or other forms of escape), and attack mode (being aggressive and bullying).

Conclusion

If the above resonates with you or is something that you would like to explore schema coaching may be for you.

Appendix I

A.1 Blank mood diary

Time	Planned action	Inner voice or emotion	Healthy adult response	Impact	Lesson learned

References

APA (2024). *What Is Exposure Therapy?*www.apa.org/ptsd-guideline/patients-and-fam ilies/exposure-therapy.

Arntz, A. (2012). Imagery rescripting as a therapeutic technique: Review of clinical trials, basic studies, and research agenda. *Journal of Experimental Psychopathology*, 3(2), 189–208.

Axelsson, E., Kern, D., Hedman-Lagerlöf, E., Lindfors, P., Palmgren, J., Hesser, H., Andersson, E., Johansson, R., Olén, O., Bonnert, M., Lalouni. M. & Ljótsson, B. (2023). Psychological treatments for irritable bowel syndrome: a comprehensive systematic review and meta-analysis. *Cognitive Behaviour Therapy*, 1–20.

Bach, B., Lockwood, G. & Young, J. E. (2018). A new look at the schema therapy model: organization and role of early maladaptive schemas. *Cognitive behaviour therapy*, 47(4), 328–349.

Bamelis, L. L., Evers, S. M., Spinhoven, P. & Arntz, A. (2014). Results of a multi-center randomized controlled trial of the clinical effectiveness of schema therapy for personality disorders. *American Journal of Psychiatry*, 171(3), 305–322.

Beck, J. S. (2011). *Cognitive behavior therapy: Basics and beyond* (2nd ed.). Guilford Press.

Beck, A. T., Rush, A. J., Shaw, B. F. & Emery, G. (1979). *Cognitive therapy of depression*. Guilford Press.

Bishop, A., Younan, R., Low, J. & Pilkington, P. D. (2022). Early maladaptive schemas and depression in adulthood: A systematic review and meta-analysis. *Clinical Psychology & Psychotherapy*, 29(1), 111–130.

Bluckert, P. (2020). *Gestalt Coaching: Distinctive Features*. Routledge.

Boyatzis, R., Smith, M. L. & Van Oosten, E. (2019). *Helping people change: Coaching with compassion for lifelong learning and growth*. Harvard Business Press.

Boyatzis, R., Liu, H., Smith, A., Zwygart, K. & Quinn, J. (2023). Competencies of coaches that predict client behavior change. *The Journal of Applied Behavioral Science*.

Brennan, D. & Wildflower, L. (2010). Ethics in coaching. In E. Cox, D. A. Clutter-buck & T. Bachkirova. (2011), *The Complete Handbook of Coaching*, pp. 369–380. Sage Publications.

Bricker, D. & Labin, M. (2012). Teaching mindfulness meditation within a schema therapy framework. *The Wiley-Blackwell Handbook of Schema Therapy: Theory, Research, and Practice*, pp. 259–270.

Britton, W. B. (2019). Can mindfulness be too much of a good thing? The value of a middle way. *Current Opinion in Psychology*, 28, 159–165.

Broder, M. S. (2000). Making optimal use of homework to enhance your therapeutic effectiveness. *Journal of rational-emotive and cognitive-behavior therapy*, 18(1), 3–18.

Brouzos, A., Vatkali, E., Mavridis, D. Vassilopoulos, S. P. & Baourda, V. C. (2022). Psychoeducation for Adults with Post-Traumatic Stress Symptomatology: A Systematic Review and Meta-Analysis. *Journal of Contemporary Psychotherapy*, 52, 155–164. doi:10.1007/s10879-021-09526-3.

Cambridge Dictionary (2023). https://dictionary.cambridge.org/us/dictionary/english/high-functioning.

Carden, J., Jones, R. J. & Passmore, J. (2023). An exploration of the role of coach training in developing self-awareness: a mixed methods study. *Current Psychology*, 42(8), 6164–6178.

Carter, J. D., McIntosh, V. V., Jordan, J., Porter, R. J., Frampton, C. M. & Joyce, P. R. (2013). Psychotherapy for depression: a randomized clinical trial comparing schema therapy and cognitive behavior therapy. *Journal of affective disorders*, 151(2), 500–505.

Castonguay, L. & Beutler, L.E. (2006). Principles of therapeutic change: a Task Force on participants, relationships, and techniques factors. *Journal of Clinical Psychology*, 62, 631–638.

Cherry, K. (2002). Key Characteristics of a Fully Functioning Person. www.verywellmind.com/fully-functioning-person-2795197#citation-4.

Cooper, M. (2008). *Essential research findings in counselling and psychotherapy*. Sage Publications.

Cooper M. & McLeod, J. (2007). A pluralistic framework for counselling and psychotherapy: Implications for research. *Journal of Counselling Psychology Research*, 7, 135–143.

Cox, E., Bachkirova, T. & Clutterbuck, D. A. (2011). *The Complete Handbook of Coaching*. Sage Publications.

Cuijpers, P., Miguel, C., Harrer, M., Plessen, C. Y., Ciharova, M., Ebert, D. & Karyotaki, E. (2023). Cognitive behavior therapy vs. control conditions, other psychotherapies, pharmacotherapies and combined treatment for depression: a comprehensive meta-analysis including 409 trials with 52,702 patients. *World Psychiatry*, 22(1), 105–115.

Curtis, R. & O'Beso, J. (2017). Pain management coaching: The missing link in the care of individuals living with chronic pain. *Journal of Applied Biobehavioral Research*, 22(4), e12082.

Dahl, V., Ramakrishnan, A., Spears, A. P., Jorge, A., Lu, J., Bigio, N. A. & Chacko, A. (2020). Psychoeducation interventions for parents and teachers of children and adolescents with ADHD: a systematic review of the literature. *Journal of Developmental and Physical Disabilities*, 32, 257–292.

Davey, G., Lake, N. & Whittington, A. (Eds). (2020). *Clinical psychology*. Routledge.

de Shazer, S., Berg, I.K., Lipchik, E., Nunnally, E., Molnar, A., Gingerich, W., Weiner- Davis, M. (1986). Brief therapy: Focused solution development. *Family Process*, 25(2), 207–221.

Dickhaut, V. & Arntz, A. (2014). Combined group and individual schema therapy for borderline personality disorder: a pilot study. *Journal of behavior therapy and experimental psychiatry*, 45(2), 242–251.

Diller, S. J., Passmore, J., Brown, H. J., Greif, S. & Jonas, E. (2020). Become the best coach you can be: the role of coach training and coaching experience in workplace coaching quality and quality control. *Organisationsberatung, Supervision, Coaching*, 27 (3), 313–333.

DiMauro, J. (2014). Exposure Therapy for Posttraumatic Stress Disorder: A Meta-Analysis, *Military Psychology*, 26(2), 120–130. doi:10.1037/mil0000038.

Dowden, C., Antonowicz, D. & Andrews, D. A. (2003). The effectiveness of relapse prevention with offenders: A meta-analysis. *International Journal of Offender Therapy and Comparative Criminology*, 47(5), 516–528.

Duman, Z. C., Yildirim, N. K., Ucok, A., Er, F. & Kanik, T. (2010). The effectiveness of a psychoeducational group program with inpatients being treated for chronic mental illness. *Social Behavior and Personality: An International Journal*, 38(5), 657-666. https://link.gale.com/apps/doc/A233502271/PPCM?u=auclib&sid=bookmark-PPCM&xid=915f5fbc.

Eadie, J., Gutierrez, G., Moghimi, E., Stephenson, C., Khalafi, P., Nikjoo, N., Jagayat, J., Gizzarelli, T., Reshetukha,. T.Omrani, M., Yang, M. & Alavi, N. (2023). Developing and implementing a web-based relapse prevention psychotherapy program for patients with alcohol use disorder: protocol for a randomized controlled trial. *JMIR Research Protocols*, 12(1), e44694.

Eftekhari, A., Ruzek, J. I., Crowley, J. J., Rosen, C. S., Greenbaum, M. A. & Karlin, B. E. (2013). Effectiveness of national implementation of prolonged exposure therapy in Veterans Affairs care. *JAMA Psychiatry*, 70(9), 949–955.

Elliott, R. (2002). The effectiveness of humanistic therapies: A meta-analysis. In D. J. Cain (Ed.), *Humanistic psychotherapies: Handbook of research and practice*, pp. 57–81. American Psychological Association. doi:10.1037/10439-002.

EMCC Global (2024). Global code of ethics: For coaches, mentors, and supervisors. https://emccuk.org/Common/Uploaded%20files/Policies/Global_Code_of_Ethics_EN_v3.pdf.

Farias, M., Maraldi, E., Wallenkampf, K. C. & Lucchetti, G. (2020). Adverse events in meditation practices and meditation-based therapies: a systematic review. *Acta Psychiatrica Scandinavica*, 142(5), 374–393.

Farrell, J. M., Shaw, I. A. & Webber, M. A. (2009). A schema-focused approach to group psychotherapy for outpatients with borderline personality disorder: a randomized controlled trial. *Journal of behavior therapy and experimental psychiatry*, 40(2), 317–328.

Foa, E., Hembree, E. A., Rothbaum, B. O. & Rauch, S. (2019). *Prolonged Exposure Therapy for PTSD: Emotional Processing of Traumatic Experiences − Therapist Guide*. Oxford University Press.

Gardiner, M., Kearns, H. & Tiggemann, M. (2013). Effectiveness of cognitive behavioural coaching in improving the well-being and retention of rural general practitioners. *Australian Journal of Rural Health*, 21(3), 183–189.

Gardner, D., McCormick, I., Forsyth, S. & Kennedy, B. (2023). Mindfulness based interventions: the good, the bad and the complicated. *New Zealand Journal of Human Resources Management*, 23(2).

Gebhardt, J. A. (2016). Quagmires for clinical psychology and executive coaching? Ethical considerations and practice challenges. *American Psychologist*, 71(3), 216.

Ghayour Kazemi, F., Shahabizadeh, F., Safara, M., Shahidsales, S., Aledavood, S. A., Hosseini, S., Taghizadeh Kermani, A. & Zarei, E. (2023). Comparing the Effectiveness of Mindfulness Based Schema Therapy and Transdiagnostic Intervention on Cognitive Fusion with Illness and Posttraumatic Avoidance in Women with

Breast Cancer: A Semi-Experimental Study. *Journal of Mazandaran University of Medical Sciences*, 33(220), 54–65.

Giesen-Bloo, J., Van Dyck, R., Spinhoven, P., Van Tilburg, W., Dirksen, C., Van Asselt, T., Kremers, I., Nadort, M. & Arntz, A. (2006). Outpatient psychotherapy for borderline personality disorder: randomized trial of schema-focused therapy vs transference-focused psychotherapy. *Archives of general psychiatry*, 63(6), 649–658.

Goldberg, S. B., Riordan, K. M., Sun, S. & Davidson, R. J. (2022). The empirical status of mindfulness-based interventions: A systematic review of 44 meta-analyses of randomized controlled trials. *Perspectives on Psychological Science*, 17(1), 108–130.

González-Ramírez, E., Carrillo-Montoya, T., García-Vega, M. L., Hart, C. E., Zavala-Norzagaray, A. A. & Ley-Quinónez, C. P. (2017). Effectiveness of hypnosis therapy and Gestalt therapy as depression treatments. *Clínica y Salud*, 28(1), 33–37.

Gorski, T. T. (1995). *Relapse prevention therapy workbook: Managing core personality and lifestyle issues*. Herald House/Independence Press.

Green, L. S., Oades, L. G. & Grant, A. M. (2006). Cognitive-behavioral, solution-focused life coaching: Enhancing goal striving, well-being, and hope. *The Journal of Positive Psychology*, 1(3), 142–149.

Green, T. C. & Balfour, A. (2020). Assessment and formulation in schema therapy. *Creative Methods in Schema Therapy Advances and Innovation in Clinical Practice*, pp. 19–47.

Greenberger, D. & Padesky, C. A. (2015). *Mind over mood: Change how you feel by changing the way you think*. Guilford Press.

Greif, S. (2018). Researching outcomes of coaching. In T. Bachkirova, G. Spence & D. Drake (Eds), *The SAGE handbook of coaching*, pp. 571–590. London: Sage Publications.

Grant, A. M. (2001). Towards a psychology of coaching. Unpublished manuscript, Sydney.

Grant, A. M. (2002). Coaching psychology. In S. J. Lopez, *The Encyclopedia of Positive Psychology*. Wiley.

Grant, A. M. (2003). The impact of life coaching on goal attainment, metacognition and mental health. *Social Behavior and personality*, 31(3), 253–264.

Grant, A.M. (2006). A personal perspective on professional coaching and the development of coaching psychology. *International Coaching Psychology Review*, 1(1).

Grant, A. M. (2017). Solution-focused cognitive–behavioral coaching for sustainable high performance and circumventing stress, fatigue, and burnout. *Consulting Psychology Journal: Practice and Research*, 69(2), 98.

Gyllensten, K. & Palmer, S. (2005). Can coaching reduce workplace stress? A quasi-experimental study. *International Journal of Evidence Based Coaching and Mentoring*, 3 (2), 75–85.

Haller, E. & Watzke, B. (2021). The role of homework engagement, homework-related therapist behaviors, and their association with depressive symptoms in telephone-based CBT for depression. *Cognitive Therapy and Research* 45, 224–235. doi:10.1007/s10608-020-10136-x.

Hayes, S.C., Strosahl, K. & Wilson, K.G. (1999). *Acceptance and commitment therapy: An experiential approach to behavior change*. Guilford Press.

Hedges, B. A. (2012). Relapse prevention workbook. https://archive.org/details/relapse-prevention-workbook.

Henley. (2024). *Henley MSc in Coaching for Behavioural Change*. www.henley.ac.uk/study/corporate-development/henley-msc-in-coaching-for-behavioural-change.

Herrera, S. N., Sarac, C., Phili, A., Gorman, J., Martin, L., Lyallpuri, R., Dobbs, M. F., DeLuca, J. S., Mueser, K. T., Wyka, K. E., Yang, L. H., Landa, Y. & Corcoran, C. M. (2023). Psychoeducation for individuals at clinical high risk for psychosis: A scoping review. *Schizophrenia Research*, 252, 148–158.

Hill, J. & Oliver, J. (2018). *Acceptance and commitment coaching: Distinctive features*. Routledge.

Hofmann, S. G., Asnaani, A., Vonk, I. J., Sawyer, A. T. & Fang, A. (2012). The efficacy of cognitive behavioral therapy: A review of meta-analyses. *Cognitive therapy and research*, 36, 427–440.

Holmes, J. & Storr, A. (2023). *The Art of Psychotherapy*. Taylor & Francis.

ICF (2023). Professional Coaching Continues Global Expansion. https://coachingfederation.org/blog/professional-coaching-continues-global-expansion.

ICF (2024). Referring a client to therapy: a set of guidelines. https://coachingfederation.org/app/uploads/2021/01/ReferringaClienttoTherapy.pdf.

Irvin, J. E., Bowers, C. A., Dunn, M. E. & Wang, M. C. (1999). Efficacy of relapse prevention: a meta-analytic review. *Journal of Consulting and Clinical Psychology*, 67(4), 563.

Jack, A. I., Passarelli, A. M. & Boyatzis, R. E. (2023). When fixing problems kills personal development: fMRI reveals conflict between Real and Ideal selves. *Frontiers in Human Neuroscience*. doi:10.3389/fnhum.2023.1128209.

Jacob, G., Van Genderen, H. & Seebauer, L. (2015). *Breaking negative thinking patterns: A schema therapy self-help and support book*. John Wiley & Sons.

James, W. (1890). *The principles of psychology* (Vol.1). Henry Holt.

Jarosz J. (2020). *Psychoeducational Role of Coaching in developing Emotional Intelligence and Well-Being*. Doctoral thesis. Katowice: Uniwersytet Śląski.

Johnsen, T. J. & Friborg, O. (2015). The effects of cognitive behavioral therapy as an anti-depressive treatment is falling: A meta-analysis. *Psychological bulletin*, 141(4), 747.

Jones, Ernest (1949). *What is Psychoanalysis?* London: Allen & Unwin.

JongsmaJr, A. E. & Bruce, T. J. (2021). *Adult psychotherapy homework planner*. John Wiley & Sons.

Kabat-Zinn, J. (1994). *Wherever you go, there you are: Mindfulness meditation in every- day life*. Hyperion Books.

Kabat-Zinn, J. (2003). Mindfulness-based interventions in context: Past, present, and future. *Clinical Psychology: Science and Practice*, 10, 144–156.

Kalantarian, E., Homaei, R. & Bozorgi, Z. D. (2024). Effects of emotional schema therapy and dialectical behavior therapy on cognitive emotion regulation in patients with bipolar II disorder. *Modern Care Journal*, 21(1).

Kazantzis, N. & Ronan, K. R. (2006). Can between-session (homework) activities be considered a common factor in psychotherapy? *Journal of Psychotherapy Integration*, 16(2), 115–127. doi:10.1037/1053-0479.16.2.115.

Kazantzis, N. & L'Abate, L. (2007). *Handbook of Homework Assignments in Psychotherapy: Research, Practice, and Prevention*. Springer.

Kazantzis, N., Whittington, C. & Dattilio, F. (2010). Meta-analysis of homework effects in cognitive and behavioral therapy: A replication and extension: homework assignments and therapy outcome. *Clinical Psychology: Science and Practice*, 17(2), 144–156. doi:10.1111/j.1468-2850.2010.01204.x.

Kazantzis, N., Whittington, C., Zelencich, L., Kyrios, M., Norton, P. J. & Hofmann, S. G. (2016). Quantity and quality of homework compliance: A meta-analysis of relations with outcome in cognitive behavior therapy. *Behavior Therapy*, 47(5), 755–772. https://doi.org/10.1016/j.beth.2016.05.002.

Kazemi, Y., Khosravi, M. & Bahonar, M. (2015). Comparing early maladaptive schemas and coping styles in drug dependent and non-dependent prisoners of Zahedan city, Iran. *Annals of Military and Health Sciences Research*, 13(1).

Kearns, H., Forbes, A. & Gardiner, M. (2007). A cognitive behavioural coaching intervention for the treatment of perfectionism and self-handicapping in a non-clinical population. *Behaviour Change*, 24(3), 157–172.

Kegan, R. (1982). *The evolving self: Problem and process in human development*. Harvard University Press.

Kellogg, S. (2015). *Transformational Chairwork: Using psychotherapeutic dialogues in clinical practice*. Rowman & Littlefield.

Khoury, B., Lecomte, T., Fortin, G., Masse, M., Therien, P., Bouchard, V., Chapleau, M.A., Paquin, K. & Hofman, S.G. (2013). Mindfulness-based therapy: A comprehensive meta-analysis. *Clinical Psychology Review*, 33(6), 763–771.

Killeen, T. K., Baker, N. L., Davis, L. L., Bowen, S. & Brady, K. T. (2023). Efficacy of mindfulness-based relapse prevention in a sample of veterans in a substance use disorder aftercare program: A randomized controlled trial. *Journal of Substance Use and Addiction Treatment*, 209116.

Kopf-Beck, J., Müller, C. L., Tamm, J., Fietz, J., Rek, N., Just, L., ... & Egli, S. (2024). Effectiveness of Schema Therapy versus Cognitive Behavioral Therapy versus Supportive Therapy for Depression in Inpatient and Day Clinic Settings: A Randomized Clinical Trial. *Psychotherapy and Psychosomatics*, 1–12.

Kuyken, W., Padesky, C. A. & Dudley, R. (2009). *Collaborative Case Conceptualization: Working Effectively with Clients*. New York: Guilford Press.

Lack, L., Wright, H & Bearpark, H. (2003). *Insomnia: How to sleep better*. ACP Publishing.

Lambert, M. J., Harmon, S. C. & Slade, K. (2007). Directions for research on homework. In A. Adhu (Ed.), *Handbook of homework assignments in psychotherapy: Research, practice, and prevention*. Springer.

Leach, S. (2022). Behavioural coaching: Theory research and practice. In *Third Wave Cognitive Behavioural Coaching: Contextual, Behavioural and Neuroscience Approaches for Evidence-based Coaches*. Pavilion Publishing and Media.

Lely, J. C., Smid, G. E., Jongedijk, R. A., W. Knipscheer, J. & Kleber, R. J. (2019). The effectiveness of narrative exposure therapy: A review, meta-analysis and meta-regression analysis. *European Journal of Psychotraumatology*, 10(1), 1550344.

Linden, W. & Hewitt, P. L. (2015). *Clinical psychology: A modern health profession*. Psychology Press.

Linehan, M. M. (1993). *Cognitive-behavioral treatment of borderline personality disorder*. Guilford Press.

Louis, J. P., Wood, A. M., Lockwood, G., Ho, M. H. R. & Ferguson, E. (2018). Positive clinical psychology and schema therapy (ST): The development of the Young Positive Schema Questionnaire (YPSQ) to complement the Young Schema Questionnaire 3 Short Form (YSQ-S3). *Psychological Assessment*, 30(9), 1199.

Levin, M. E., Navarro, C., Cruz, R. A. & Haeger, J. (2019). Comparing in-the-moment skill coaching effects from tailored versus non-tailored acceptance and commitment therapy mobile apps in a non-clinical sample. *Cognitive Behaviour Therapy*, 48(3), 200–216.

Lockwood, G. & Perris, P. (2012). A new look at core emotional needs. In *The Wiley-Blackwell handbook of schema therapy: Theory, research, and practice*, pp. 41–66.

Lungu, A., Boone, M. S., Chen, S. Y., Chen, C. E. & Walser, R. D. (2021). Effectiveness of a cognitive behavioral coaching program delivered via video in real world settings. *Telemedicine and e-Health*, 27(1), 47–54.

Mann, D. (2020). *Gestalt therapy: 100 key points and techniques*. Routledge.

Marchena Giráldez, C. A., Froxán Parga, M. X. & Calero Elvira, A. (2023). Homework assignment and compliance review from a behavioural perspective: the verbal sequences between therapist and client. *Behavioral Psychology/Psicología Conductual*, *31(1)*, 111–127. doi:10.51668/bp.8323107n.

Mao, L., Li, P., Wu, Y., Luo, L. & Hu, M. (2023). The effectiveness of mindfulness-based interventions for ruminative thinking: A systematic review and meta-analysis of randomized controlled trials. *Journal of Affective Disorders*, 321, 83–95.

Malogiannis, I.A., Arntz, A., Spyropoulou, A., Tsartsara, E., Aggeli, A., Karveli, S., Vlavianou, M., Pehlivanidis, A., Papadimitriou, G. N. & Zervas I. (2014) Schema therapy for patients with chronic depression: a single case series study. *Journal of Behavioral Therapy and Experimental Psychiatry*, 45, 319–329.

Mansourzadeh, A., Shaygannejad, V., Mirmosayyeb, O., Afshari-Safavi, A. & Gay, M. C. (2024). Effectiveness of Schema Therapy on Anxiety, Depression, Fatigue, Quality of Life, and Sleep in Patients with Multiple Sclerosis: A Randomized Controlled Trial. *Middle East Journal of Rehabilitation and Health Studies*, 11(1).

Marlatt, G. A. & Witkiewitz, K. (2005). Relapse prevention for alcohol and drug problems. *Relapse prevention: Maintenance strategies in the treatment of addictive behaviors*, 2, 1–44.

Mausbach, B. T., Moore, R., Roesch, S., Cardenas, V. & Patterson, T. L. (2010). An updated meta-analysis: The relationship between homework compliance and therapy outcomes. *Cognitive Therapy and Research*, 34(5), 429–438. doi:10.1007/s10608-010-9297-z.

Maxwell, A. (2009). The co-created boundary: negotiating the limits of coaching. *International Journal of Evidence Based Coaching & Mentoring* (Special Issue No. 3, November), 82–94.

McCormick, I.A. (2022). Schema coaching: Theory, research and practice. In J. Passmore & S. Leach (Eds), *Third Wave Cognitive Behavioural Coaching: Contextual, Behavioural and Neuroscience Approaches for Evidence-based Coaches*. Pavilion Publishing and Media.

McCormick, I. A. (2023a). An introduction to schema coaching techniques, part 1: The schema octagon. *The Coaching Psychologist*, 19(1), 26–32.

McCormick, I. A. (2023b). Case conceptualisation using schema coaching analysis: an illustrative case study. *Coaching Psychology International*, 16(9), 1–7.

McCormick, I. A. (2023c). Schema coaching techniques, part 2: Schema case conceptualisation and psychoeducation. *The Coaching Psychologist*, 19(2), 4–12.

McCormick, I. A. (in press). Schema coaching techniques, part 3: Imagery rescripting and transformational chairwork. In *The Coaching Psychologist*.

McCormick, I. A. (2023d). Schema coaching techniques, part 4: Schema challenge cards and mindful release [Unpublished manuscript]. Auckland: McCormick Executive Coach.

McCormick, I. A. & Forsyth, S. (in press). Assessing the effectiveness of group based reflective practice for coaches. *International Journal of Evidence Based Coaching and Mentoring*.

McLean, C. P., Levy, H. C., Miller, M. L. & Tolin, D. F. (2021). Exposure therapy for PTSD: A meta-analysis. *Clinical psychology review*, 102115.

McKay, S. & Kemp, T. (2018). Neuroscience and coaching: A practical application. In *Positive Psychology Coaching in Practice*, pp. 57–67. Routledge.

McMahon, G. (2011). *No More Stress! Be your Own Stress Management Coach*. Routledge.

Melemis, S. M. (2015). Focus: addiction: relapse prevention and the five rules of recovery. *The Yale Journal of Biology and Medicine*, 88(3), 325.

Merriam-Webster (2021). The online dictionary. www.merriam-webster.com/dictionary.

Moone, N. & Glenister, J. (2017). Case Conceptualisation. *Psychosocial Assessment in Mental Health*, 185.

Moreno, J. L. (1946). *Psychodrama* (Vol. 1). Beacon House.

Morina, N., Kampmann, I., Emmelkamp, P., Barbui, C. & Hoppen, T. H. (2023). Meta-analysis of virtual reality exposure therapy for social anxiety disorder. *Psychological Medicine*, 53(5), 2176–2178.

Nadort, M., Arntz, A., Smit, J. H., Giesen-Bloo, J., Eikelenboom, M., Spinhoven, P., van Asselt, T., Wensing, M. & van Dyck, M. (2009) v *Behaviour Research and Therapy*, 47, 961–973.

Neenan, M. & Dryden, W. (2020). *Cognitive behavioural coaching: A guide to problem solving and personal development*. Routledge.

Neenan, M. & Palmer, S. (Eds). (2021). *Cognitive behavioural coaching in practice: An evidence based approach*. Routledge.

Nehra, D. K., Sharma, N. R., Kumar, P. & Nehra, S. (2013). Mindfulness based stress reduction: An overview. In D. Hooda & N. R. Sharma (Eds), *Mental health risk and resources*, pp. 197–231. Global Vision.

Nehra, D. K., Sharma, N. R., Kumar, P. & Nehra, S. (2013). Mindfulness based stress reduction: An overview. In D. Hooda & N. R. Sharma (Eds), *Mental health risk and resources*, pp. 197–231. Global Vision.

Noel, M., Palermo, T. M., Chambers, C. T., Taddio, A. & Hermann, C. (2015). Remembering the pain of childhood: Applying a developmental perspective framework to the study of pain memories. *PAIN*, 156(1), 31–34. doi:10.1016/j.pain.0000000000000001.

Nordahl, H. M. & Nysæter, T. E. (2005). Schema therapy for patients with borderline personality disorder: A single case series. *Journal of Behavior Therapy and Experimental Psychiatry*, 36(3), 254–264.

Palmer, S. & McMahon, G. (Eds). (1997). *Handbook of counselling*. Routledge.

Palmer, S. & Szymanska, K. (2018). Cognitive behavioural coaching: An integrative approach. In *Handbook of coaching psychology*, pp. 108–127. Routledge.

Passmore, J. & Leach, S. (2022). *Third wave cognitive behavioural coaching: contextual, behavioural and neuroscience approaches for evidence based coaches*. Pavilion Publishing and Media.

Passmore, J & Leach, S. (2022). Introduction: second wave cognitive behavioural approaches. In *Third Wave Cognitive Behavioural Coaching: Contextual, Behavioural and Neuroscience Approaches for Evidence-based Coaches*. Pavilion Publishing and Media.

Passmore, J. & Oades, L. G. (2015) Positive psychology techniques: positive case conceptualisation. *The Coaching Psychologist*, 11(1) 43–45. http://centaur.reading.ac.uk/81942.

Peeters, N., van Passel, B. & Krans, J. (2022). The effectiveness of schema therapy for patients with anxiety disorders, OCD, or PTSD: A systematic review and research agenda. *British Journal of Clinical Psychology*, 61(3), 579–597.

Peliquin, S. (2023). A Client's Guide to Schema-Focused Cognitive Therapy. www.sallypeloquinpsychology.com.au/uploads/1/6/3/0/16303604/client_guide-schema_therapy.pdf.

Perls, F. S. (1969). *Gestalt Therapy Verbatim*. Reprinted by Gestalt Journal Press.

Prevatt, F. & Yelland, S. (2015). An empirical evaluation of ADHD coaching in college students. *Journal of attention disorders*, 19(8), 666–677.

Pollio, D. E., North, C. S., Reid, D. L., Miletic, M. M. & McClendon, J. R. (2006). Living with severe mental illness–what families and friends must know: evaluation of a one-day psychoeducation workshop. *Social Work*, 51(1), 31–38. https://link.gale.com/apps/doc/A143163712/PPCM?u=auclib&sid=bookmark-PPCM&xid=d66f4ade.

Powell, L. A., Parker, J., Weighall, A. & Harpin, V. (2022). Psychoeducation Intervention Effectiveness to Improve Social Skills in Young People with ADHD: A Meta-Analysis. *Journal of attention disorders*, 26(3), 340–357.

Pugh, M. & Broome, N. (2020). Dialogical coaching: An experiential approach to personal and professional development. *Consulting Psychology Journal: Practice and Research*, 72(3), 223.

Rafaeli, E., Bernstein, D. P. & Young, J. (2011). *Schema Therapy: Distinctive Features*. Routledge.

Raffagnino, R. (2019). Gestalt Therapy Effectiveness: A Systematic Review of Empirical Evidence. *Open Journal of Social Sciences*, 7, 66–83. doi:10.4236/jss.2019.76005.

Reger, G. M., Hoffman, J., Riggs, D., Rothbaum, B. O., Ruzek, J., Holloway, K. M. & Kuhn, E. (2013). The "PE coach" smartphone application: An innovative approach to improving implementation, fidelity, and homework adherence during prolonged exposure. *Psychological services*, 10(3), 342.

Reiss, N., Lieb, K., Arntz, A., Shaw, I. A. & Farrell, J. (2014). Responding to the treatment challenge of patients with severe BPD: Results of three pilot studies of inpatient schema therapy. *Behavioural and Cognitive Psychotherapy*, 42(3), 355–367.

Renner, F., Arntz, A., Leeuw, I. & Huibers, M. (2013). Treatment for chronic depression using schema therapy. *Clinical Psychology: Science and Practice*, 20(2), 166.

Riggenbach, J. (2012). *The CBT toolbox: A workbook for clients and clinicians*. PESI Publishing & Media.

Riso, L. P., Froman, S. E., Raouf, M., Gable, P., Maddux, R. E., Turini-Santorelli, N., Penna, S., Blandino, J. A., Jacobs, C. H. & Cherry, M. (2006). The long-term stability of early maladaptive schemas. *Cognitive Therapy and Research*, 30, 515–529.

Robberegt, S. J., Brouwer, M. E., Kooiman, B. E., Stikkelbroek, Y. A., Nauta, M. H. & Bockting, C. L. (2023). Meta-analysis: relapse prevention strategies for depression and anxiety in remitted adolescents and young adults. *Journal of the American Academy of Child & Adolescent Psychiatry*, 62(3), 306–317.

Rodolico, A., Bighelli, I., Avanzato, C., Concerto, C., Cutrufelli, P., Mineo, L. & Leucht, S. (2022). Family interventions for relapse prevention in schizophrenia: a systematic review and network meta-analysis. *The Lancet Psychiatry*.

Roediger, E., Stevens, B. A. & Brockman, R. (2018) *Contextual Schema Therapy: An integrative approach to personality disorders, emotional dysregulation, and interpersonal functioning*. New Harbinger Publications.

Rogers, C. R. (1962). Toward becoming a fully functioning person. In A. W. Combs (Ed.), *Perceiving, behaving, becoming: A new focus for education*, pp. 21–33. National Education Association. doi:10.1037/14325-003.

Ryum, T., Bennion, M. & Kazantzis, N. (2023). Integrating between-session homework in psychotherapy: A systematic review of immediate in-session and intermediate outcomes. *Psychotherapy*, 60(3), 306–319. doi:10.1037/pst0000488.

Sala, M., Keshishian, A., Song, S., Moskowitz, R., Bulik, C. M., Roos, C. R. & Levinson, C. A. (2023). Predictors of relapse in eating disorders: A meta-analysis. *Journal of Psychiatric Research*.

Segal, Z.V., Williams, J.M.G & Teasdale, J.D. (2002). *Mindfulness-based cognitive therapy for depression*. Guilford Press.

Shapiro, S. L., Carlson, L. E., Astin, J. A. & Freedman, B. (2006). Mechanisms of mindfulness. *Journal of clinical psychology*, 62(3), 373–386.

Sharma, A. K., Shadakshari, D., Chand, P. & Murthy, P. (2023). Design, development and pilot testing of 'Quest', a smartphone-based relapse prevention app for patients with alcohol dependence. *Asian journal of psychiatry*, 83, 103572.

Shojaadini, E. & Saeid, Y. A. (2019). Relationship between early maladaptive schemas and attachment styles in prisoners with borderline personality disorder in Hamadan prison center. *Military Caring Sciences Journal*, 5(3), 220–227.

Siehl, S., Robjant, K. & Crombach A. (2021). Systematic review and meta-analyses of the long-term efficacy of narrative exposure therapy for adults, children and perpetrators. *Psychotherapy Research*, 31(6), 695–710. doi:10.1080/10503307.2020.1847345.

Simon, L., Steinmetz, L., Feige, B., Benz, F., Spiegelhalder, K. & Baumeister, H. (2023). Comparative efficacy of onsite, digital, and other settings for cognitive behavioral therapy for insomnia: a systematic review and network meta-analysis. *Scientific Reports*, 13(1), 1929.

Simpson, S. & Arntz, A. (2020). Core principles of imagery. In G. Heath & H. Startup (Eds), *Creative methods in Schema therapy: advances and innovation in clinical practice*. Routledge.

Słysz, A. & Soroko, E. (2021). How do Psychotherapists Develop a Case Conceptualisation? Thematic Analysis of Conceptual Maps. *Journal of Contemporary Psychotherapy*, 51(2), 87–96.

Stanier, M. B. (2016). *The coaching habit: Say less, ask more & change the way you lead forever*. Box of Crayons Press.

Skews, R. 2018. Acceptance and commitment therapy (ACT) informed coaching: Examining outcomes and mechanisms of change. Doctoral thesis, Goldsmiths, University of London.

Swift, J. K. & Parkin, S. R. (2017). The client as the expert in psychotherapy: What clinicians and researchers can learn about treatment processes and outcomes from psychotherapy clients. *Journal of Clinical Psychology*, 73(11), 1486–1488. doi:10.1002/jclp.22528.

Szabó, P. & Meier, D. (2009). *Coaching Plain and Simple: Solution Focused Brief Coaching Essentials*. W.W. Norton & Company.

Tay, K. C. P., Seow, C. C. D., Xiao, C., Lee, H. M. J., Chiu, H. F. & Chan, S. W. C. (2016). Structured interviews examining the burden, coping, self-efficacy, and quality of life among family caregivers of persons with dementia in Singapore. *Dementia*, 15(2), 204–220.

Thera, N. (2005). *The heart of buddhist meditation: Satipaṭṭhāna: A handbook of mental training based on the Buddha's way of mindfulness, with an anthology of relevant texts translated from the Pali and Sanskrit.* Buddhist Publication Society.

Tomoiagă, C. & David, O. (2023). Is cognitive-behavioral coaching an empirically supported approach to coaching? a meta-analysis to investigate its outcomes and moderators. *Journal of Rational-Emotive & Cognitive-Behavior Therapy*, 1–22.

Van Dam, N. T., Van Vugt, M. K., Vago, D. R., Schmalzl, L., Saron, C. D., Olendzki, A., Meissner, T., Lazar, S. W., Kerr, C. E., Gorchov, J., Fox, K. C. R., Field, B. A., Britton, W. B., Brefczynski-Lewis, J. A. & Meyer, D. E. (2018). Mind the hype: A critical evaluation and prescriptive agenda for research on mindfulness and meditation. *Perspectives on psychological science*, 13(1), 36–61.

Van Vreeswijk, M., Broersen, J. & Schurink, G. (2014). *Mindfulness and schema therapy: A practical guide.* John Wiley & Sons.

Videler, A. C., Rossi, G., Schoevaars, M., Van Der Feltz-Cornelis, C. M. & Van Alphen, S. P. J. (2014). Effects of schema group therapy in older outpatients: a proof of concept study. *International Psychogeriatrics*, 26(10), 1709–1717.

Videler, A. C., van Royen, R. J., Legra, M. J. & Ouwens, M. A. (2020). Positive schemas in schema therapy with older adults: clinical implications and research suggestions. *Behavioural and cognitive psychotherapy*, 48(4), 481–491.

Unterecker, S. (2019). Compliance and psychoeducation. *NeuroPsychopharmacotherapy*, 1–9. doi:10.1007/978-3-319-56015-1_6-1.

Walker, J. (2004). Business-class coaches. *Business Review Weekly*, 1 July, 15–18.

Weatherhead (2024). Foundations of Coaching Certificate from Weatherhead School of Management. https://execed.case.edu/public/category/courseCategoryCertificateProfile.do?method=load&certificateId=1957696&certificateName=foundations-of-coaching-certificate.

Wikipedia (2024a). Coaching. https://en.wikipedia.org/wiki/Coaching.

Wikipedia (2024b). Global Assessment of Functioning. https://en.wikipedia.org/wiki/Global_Assessment_of_Functioning.

Williams, C. (2012). *Overcoming Anxiety, Stress and Panic: A Five Areas Approach.* Routledge.

Xia, J., Merinder, L. B. & Belgamwar, M. R. (2011). Psychoeducation for schizophrenia. *Schizophrenia Bulletin*, 37, 21–22.

Young, J. E., Klosko, J. S. & Weishaar, M. E. (2003). *Schema therapy: a practitioner's guide.* Guilford Press.

Young, J. E. & Klosko, J. S. (1994). *Reinventing your life: The breakthrough program to end negative behavior… and feel great again.* Penguin.

Zeng, X., Chiu, C. P., Wang, R., Oei, T. P. & Leung, F. Y. (2015). The effect of loving-kindness meditation on positive emotions: a meta-analytic review. *Frontiers in psychology*, 6, 1693.

Index for Schema Coaching

Printed in the United States
by Baker & Taylor Publisher Services